A SPECIAL NOTE

Today young men are fighting battles, both physically and spiritually, on every continent of our world. I salute those who courageously stand for freedom and truth. The American military who have served in Operation Desert Storm have my highest respect and deepest appreciation. Copies of the book you hold in your hands were sent to more than 15,000 of those troops, free, by friends who cared enough to invest in their lives.

But a potentially greater, more disastrous, war rages in full-blown fury. From the streets of Brooklyn to the mountains of Oregon, men are fighting the war waged against them by the enemy of their souls, the very enemy of God. Young men around the globe are being assaulted by deadly and demonic forces. It is true — Satan himself has declared war on the men of this generation.

More than ever before in history, young men of today must be trained to be men, and have the courage to live in that manhood.

This book is about manhood and courage.

COURAGE

Winning Life's Toughest Battles

Special Limited Edition

by
Edwin Louis Cole

Harrison House
Tulsa, Oklahoma

Unless otherwise indicated,
all Scripture quotations are taken from
the *King James Version* of the Bible.

Some Scripture quotations are taken from *The Living Bible.* Copyright © 1971 by Tyndale House Publishers, Wheaton, Illinois.

15th Printing
Over 227,000 in Print

COURAGE — Winning Life's Toughest Battles
Special Limited Edition
ISBN 0-89274-873-7
(Formerly ISBN 0-89274-362-X)

Edwin Louis Cole Ministries
International Headquarters
P. O. Box 610588
Dallas, TX 75261

West Coast Offices
P. O. Box 626
Corona del Mar, CA 92625

Published by Harrison House, Inc.
P. O. Box 35035
Tulsa, Oklahoma 74153

Printed in the United States of America.

DEDICATION

This book, though devoted to men who desire to be champions, is dedicated to three people who are.

Paul Louis Cole
Lois Cole Bivins
Joann Webster

CONTENTS

Introduction

1 "Despise Not Thy Youth" 13

2 Courage 25

3 WIMPS: Made In America 41

4 Sex 57

5 How Do You Spell "Release"? 73

6 The Invisible Man 89

7 Working Hard, Going Nowhere 105

8 Bend, Bow or Burn 117

9 Write It on Your Shorts 135

10 CHAMPIONS: Men Who Never Quit 155

ACKNOWLEDGMENTS

My sincere thanks to:

. . . the Harrison House editors for their help in producing this book.

. . . my daughter, Joann Webster, without whose time and tireless efforts, this book could not have been possible.

INTRODUCTION

For four years I had been criss-crossing America ministering to men. It was the most satisfying work I had ever done in my life. But in the midst of preparing for the greatest event in the years of ministry to that point, the first National Christian Men's Event, I realized something was missing. As the days went by the missing element finally became clear.

For years before this as I prepared for each new year, a new emphasis and direction was impressed upon me by the Lord in December. It was as though God had a divine timetable and wanted it fulfilled. In His faithfulness, He prepared me for the next step year after year.

The pattern started in 1976 when He gave me five words which would be the basis for starting a ministry that majored in men:

- *Sanctify* yourself.
- *Preach* the Word.

- *Go* doubting nothing.
- *Use* the gold, but don't touch the glory.
- *Pray* this prayer: "Grant to thy servant great boldness in preaching, send forth your healing power, and may signs, wonders and miracles be done in the name of your Holy Servant Jesus," from Acts 4:29.

In successive years the Lord would add to these, establishing a pattern and emphasizing what was to come next.

For four years in this ministry to men I watched men in action. I had worked with, ministered to, and counselled with men for years as a senior pastor, on television and radio, and in various aspects of ministry. As I continued this while moving in the new direction God was leading me, there was a fresh constant flow of truth, insights, information and understanding that was changing men's lives by the thousands.

Just months before that first National Christian Men's Event, in December, God revealed to me what was missing. The new emphasis for the ministry was to teach young men to become identified with what God wanted to do in their lives as *men*. The result of this became known as Project Timothy, an outreach named after the young man who so loved truth, that he became a special project to the Apostle Paul who determined to see him become a great man of God.

The goal of Project Timothy today is to reach young men in their teens and early twenties with the truth that "Manhood and Christlikeness are synonymous."

To some, that won't seem young at all. A Jewish boy is readied for manhood for four years before his Bar Mitzvah at age 13—when he is considered to be entering manhood.

Pornographers have adopted the philosophy that if a child is hooked when he is young, when he is old he will not depart from it. According to magazine sources, the smut peddlers now are aiming at 11 year olds. One of the greatest money-making schemes in the movie industry today is the teenage sex film.

What was happening in my ministry was that in announcing "Men's Meetings," very few high school and college men were attending. I was speaking mainly to married men or older singles who perhaps had been married.

What was bothering me had finally come to light.

Throughout our nation, especially in churches, young men in high school are called "youths." When entering college, they are referred to as "young adults."

They're not called "men."

Just "youths." And "young adults."

No wonder young women today ask, "Where are all the men?" Young men don't think of themselves as men because they have never been called "men."

So, when a "Men's Meeting" is announced, the young men stay home.

There were almost 8,000 of us at Hofheinz Pavilion on the University of Houston campus for the National Christian Men's Event. All men.

It had been a great day, and we were reaching a peak moment. Because the Lord made us recognize the absence of young men in our meetings, we had begun our Project Timothy effort to bring them to this men's event.

The final call that day was a challenge directed at the young men.

"Aren't there any young men of high school or college age that have the guts or courage to do more than wallow around in the moral morass of mediocrity to which so many have sunk?

"Isn't there any young man anywhere who wants to be a champion for God? Have they all succumbed to the world?

"Isn't there anyone anywhere who wants to stand up for God, admit that he wants to be a 'Man of God' and pay the price of championship by developing a godly character?

"If there is...."

Before the statement could be finished, hundreds of young men leaped from their chairs and began to run for the front, some jumping the walls on the bottom of that basketball arena to race to center court where they stood, 400 strong, declaring their allegiance to Jesus Christ.

As they ran, the other men stood and applauded them, some of them weeping as they watched these young men who were not ashamed to be called "Men of God."

It was explosive.

One young man, in the intensity of the moment, threw his bag of cocaine on the platform. Others threw things from their pockets that signified their rejection of the uncleanness in their lives.

Thank God there are young men who have that burning desire to be outstanding ...men who are willing to pay the price for the true manhood which is Christlikeness ...single men who realize they need to grow and mature as men *now,* not wait until they are married.

Thank God for you, as you read this book.

You may not have an aisle to run down, or a wall to leap over, or a platform to stand in front of, but at least right now you can finish this sentence, lay down the book and look toward God as you admit your desire to become a MAN OF GOD.

"DESPISE NOT THY YOUTH"

1

"DESPISE NOT THY YOUTH"

This is not a book of "how to."

It is a book of "why not?"

This book is not a manual for living.

It is an exhortation to live.

I'm writing it to tell you:

"YOU ARE A MAN!"

Don't waste your youth.

The strength of your youth is your glory.

Don't let anyone despise it.

But don't let them take your manhood, either.

Joseph was 17 when God gave him the dream that would be his life's motivation and was prophetically fulfilled by the Lord later in life.

David was a teenager when he faced the giant Goliath. Daniel and his three Hebrew friends were about that same age when they determined to make a stand for God before the Babylonian king.

Our Lord Jesus Christ was only 12 when we have a glimpse of Him in the Temple and hear Him saying that He must be about His Father's business while confounding the teachers with His wisdom.

There are advantages in youth that allow for great things to be done. Strength is one advantage.

Never be ashamed of your youth.

Acknowledge it.

Channel it.

Use it.

Turn it toward God and revel in it.

Sure, some men are late bloomers. But there is a great advantage to the fertile mind, the quick ability to learn, the ready molding of character, and physical energy which never can be recaptured later in life. You must realize and capitalize on those qualities, and refuse to let an intimidating world hinder you.

I don't wonder that modern man has problems, is confused, drained of morals and dead in spirit. It's a marvel he isn't worse off. Look at what men have had to contend with during the last few years.

Consider the array of forces of every kind and description battling for your mind, soul and body.

Sexists, communists, psychologists, humanists, cultists, religionists, hedonists, geneticists, satanists, pacifists and all other kinds of "ists."

Is it any wonder that some men are confused?

Add to that the daily barrage of music blasting at men, dulling their sensibilities, seducing their spirits and hampering them mentally, physically, culturally and spiritually.

Look at what you've been up against.

The so-called "Me Generation" is the product of a modern philosophy advocating a lifestyle that says, "If it feels good—do it."

That philosophy has sown many of the seeds of anarchy, rebellion and rioting in our world.

For years there has been what is known as the "antihero" syndrome at work in our society. Its product was a textbook genocide that killed off heroes and even patriotism for at least a decade.

A new "species" of man has developed from these trends.

"Wimps—Made in America" are the modern men who are unable to appreciate their own masculinity, who are insecure, inferior, insipid and inadequate.

From another angle, a barrage of intimidation was leveled at men labeling them "male chauvinist pigs." Soft males and hard females decry the male image. Women's Lib started out rightfully as a rejection of men's double standards, extremes of attitudes and ignorance of responsibility, but degenerated into a rebellion unleashing the fury of its hostility against manhood.

Gay rights advocates present an image that to them represents manhood at its finest. How pitiful!

Single-parent households, with only a mother and no father figure at home, raise young men without a male role model or male discipline. Subconscious resentments built up toward an absentee father are often manifested in anarchistic behavior toward authority in the classroom and community.

A recent article revealed that most assassination attempts were made by men and women who had not had a father at home. No wonder the absentee father is the curse of our day.

Today's androgynous appeal is the result of yesterday's unisex efforts. But the blending of male and female results in gender castration.

Michael Jackson, on his "Victory Tour," was hailed as the epitome of the new androgynous man. He may be a great performer and musical genius, but he is far from many people's idea of an ideal man.

During the past decades the media often have presented fathers as bumbling idiots, marriage as warfare and women as sex objects, while heroes were old fashioned and most male characters could only resolve conflict through violence.

For years men have been bombarded from every side, and the beating took its toll. Men either gave in to, abandoned or lashed out at women. Their frustration has resulted in efforts to legalize incest, feature rape in movies, exploit women in pornography and depict rape victims as villains.

Even in the Church there are problems.

The tendency has been for pastors to pontificate, youth pastors to placate, and elders to create cynicism or give undue criticism to young people.

Priests minister from the people to the Lord, while prophets minister from the Lord to the people. Men need to be able to function in both roles as God directs them.

Our world needs prophets.

Prophets desire to emphasize that specific word or truth given to them. But they would be unbalanced without pastors. Pastors balance the truth with the total life of their congregations.

The great tragedy so often is when pastors reject the revelation rather than refine it.

There is a difference between being a covering and being a lid.

Listen to me. If you, as a young man, want to live a powerful and victorious life for God, but you are attending meetings led by a pablum-preaching, placebo-praying youth pastor whose only concern is his status before the senior minister or gratifying his ego before the girls — then find another place to worship.

If you are a youth pastor and are offended by that, it's too bad. All you have to do is change, ask God to forgive you, and you won't be offended anymore.

Many youth pastors are only concerned about the Big Three: recreation, entertainment, and social activities with their groups.

They would be much happier working as cruise directors on some ship — and probably would get more done.

Intercessory prayer, the exercise of faith, witnessing and intensive study of the Word all seem to suffer from indifference or unbelief with these men. They seem to care more about status symbols than spirituality.

Young men need the meat of the Word, not mush.

The commission is to make disciples as Jesus did — to train by example.

Thank God, though, there are some pastors and youth pastors who have a godly concern for the discipling process and make every effort to achieve it. What a refreshing joy to find such men and associate with them!

If your pastor is one like that, get next to him, learn from him, let him disciple you. It's God's plan.

Senior pastors also need to realize that discipling their youth pastor as a "Timothy" is their God-given trust and responsibility. Too often, senior pastors feel threatened by the success of the younger man and the old "Saul Syndrome" goes to work.

The "Saul Syndrome" is my description of the Biblical account of King Saul's attitude toward King David. It says that when the people sang the praises of the two men they sang of Saul overcoming thousands, but David overcoming *ten*-thousands. Saul's pride could not admit that David had greater exploits, and his jealousy turned both venomous and murderous.

He could not stand the younger man doing greater exploits than he had done.

Contrast that with the relationship between Paul and Timothy. Paul recognized the great potential in Timothy and determined not only to teach him, but to train and disciple him to become a great man of God.

Senior pastors must realize that discipling a young man to do greater things than they have done is a glory to them, not a threat.

Youth pastors and associates need to learn that when a senior pastor has the desire to disciple them and give them the benefit of his years of experience, it isn't a time for usurping and undermining his authority as Absolom did to his father, King David.

The characteristics of a kingdom emanate from the character of the king.

This is true in a nation, church, classroom, home, sports team.

The characteristics of a congregation emanate from the character of the pastor. Like begets like.

A pastor whose characteristic is the love of the truth will have a congregation that loves the truth.

This is one of the principles God gives in His Word, on which you can base your life: like begets like. God has given you the power to overcome any obstacle, enemy or attack through the truth of His patterns and principles.

It's God's desire for you to know His patterns and principles.

It's your right to know the truth.

Every man needs to understand the pattern in the parable of the prodigal son. It contains regenerative principles that are life changing.

The prodigal son demanded his inheritance from his father then squandered it foolishly on personal pleasure. He is a perfect example of the high cost of low living. In his moment of desperation, when he had lost everything, the only place he could turn was to a father's love and dependence upon his mercy. Through the faithfulness of his father, he was saved from the devastation of his own folly.

The pattern Jesus gave us in the parable is:

- Rebellion
- Ruin
- Repentance
- Reconciliation
- Restoration

The pivotal point between ruin and reconciliation is repentance. That has never changed. It's an eternal truth.

The prodigal began his ruin with two words: "Give me." He cared not that he broke his mother's heart, denied his father's will, and rejected his brother's affection.

Sin never cares about anything except gratifying its own desires. It pays no heed to consequences.

"Make me" were the words that changed his life.

They showed his submission to authority, his willingness to change, and an acceptance of personal responsibility for his actions. That's the beginning of real manhood.

God will move heaven and earth for that man.

God came from heaven to earth for that man.

Are you ready to be that man?

COURAGE

2
COURAGE

The meeting was jammed with men. Many were young, single, good-looking men of high school and college age. Three of them on the front row of the second section caught my eye.

All three came in together and sat together. One listened intently to the message while the other two whispered, smirked and quietly joked with each other.

I almost stopped speaking to tell those "turkeys" to shut up, but I didn't.

At the end, the call was given for young men who wanted to be champions in the Kingdom of God, who were willing to make a wholehearted, single-eyed dedication to the Lord, men who had the courage to be different and admit their desire to be a *Man of God.* One of those three young men slowly and deliberately stood to his feet. His friends sat sullenly, silently and insolently.

Self-righteous, self-justified and hardened of heart, the "church-wise" kids are deceived in their way as much as the "street-wise" kids are in theirs. They need the smirk pulled off their faces, the insolence off their spirits and the veneer off their lives.

In contrast to the self-righteous kids was the one who broke away that night to become his own man. His independent act of courage so stirred me that I addressed him for the whole crowd to hear.

"Son, I commend you for what you have just done. You did not allow yourself to be intimidated by the peer pressure of your friends, but you made your own individual decision and did it openly and honestly before everyone. In my book, sir, you are a man."

The audience broke out in spontaneous applause as they recognized what he had done. His life changed that night.

He had reverence for God. His buddies sneered.

He submitted to righteousness. They rejected it.

After the meeting, I saw an older man walk over to him and put his arms around those young shoulders. The young man hugged him without embarrassment. After they embraced, the older man came to me and said, "That's my son."

The son had what it takes—courage.

The "church-wise" show no courage.

A mother told me she sent her daughter to an overnight outing with the church youth group, hoping her daughter would experience a spiritual renewal in her relationship with the Lord. Instead, her daughter came home distraught, distressed and depressed.

Some of the "church-wise" young men had grabbed her physically, demeaning her with their brutish advances. They pointed her out and laughed among themselves, while the youth pastor was busy setting up the movie filled with suggestive sex that was his planned social activity for the evening. How sad.

These same "church-wise" young men earlier had visited a convalescent hospital to "witness" to the elderly. Projecting personality, polished in their performance, going through the motions of their religion—these guys are just con artists.

Playing the game.

God looks on the heart, not the facade.

If you are in that kind of "church-wise" group, or if you have friends like that, but you want to be a man of God—*then get away from them.* Have nothing to do with them. Their deception is dangerous to your dedication to God.

You must add courage to your faith.

It takes courage to resist the peer pressure of your friends—courage not to go with the crowd.

It takes courage to face reality.

Courage to admit need.

Courage to change.

Courage to make decisions.

Courage to hold convictions.*

Success is not based on the ability to say yes, but on the ability to say no.

Ask any successful man or woman. Ask anyone with honor or virtue who elicits your respect. They will tell you they learned how to say no.

However, courage and firmness must be directed by knowledge. You must know what is right in order to know what to resist and what to yield to.

---

*Edwin Louis Cole, *The Potential Principle* (Springdale: Whitaker House, 1984), p.21.

A recent television campaign against drugs is based on popularizing the truth that it is both right and courageous to say no to drug use.

Courage can be the virtue of the wise or the vanity of fools.

It takes courage to stand your ground. But it takes courage coupled with wisdom to know when to run.

In Genesis, chapter 39, Potiphar's wife tried to seduce Joseph, but he turned and fled. It took courage to run. That's why Paul wrote to Timothy and said, "Flee also youthful lusts."

The foolish man would have said, "I can stay here and not give in." The wise man knew when to flee.

Moral courage enables a person to encounter hatred, disapproval and contempt without departing from what is right.

Moral cowardice causes a person to shrink from duty and danger, to dread pain and harm, to yield to fear.

Moral cowardice is the ruin of manhood.

Double-minded men waver between right and wrong. Because they are undecided, they constantly are tempted to yield to evil. They profess to hate sin, but have a lingering love for it. As a result, they do not have a right understanding of good and evil, which is absolutely necessary to battle the world, the lusts of the flesh and the devil.

Rob is a young man I've known off and on for a number of years. When he makes a commitment to the Lord, he comes around to see me. When it wears off, he stays away.

Rob had a close relationship with the Lord when he was in high school and showed a tremendous capacity for leadership. But after being rejected by his mother because of his Christian faith, and being rejected by a Christian girlfriend because he did not control his youthful lusts, he believed he had to prove himself to women. He became double-minded.

He says he loves the Lord in his heart, yet he wallows in promiscuity, lewd behavior and addictions. He is unproductive in his work, can't find a steady girlfriend who satisfies him and swings constantly from one extreme to another. He is unstable in all his ways.

To top it off, he rationalizes his failures because of what happened with his mother and girlfriend in high school. Rob will never be a success until he decides who he is going to serve—God or himself. It will take courage.

The Bible is a book of moral courage.

John the Baptist had it when he rebuked the king for his sin.

David added it to his faith when he stood before Goliath.

Daniel needed it in his decision not to eat the king's food that had been offered to idols. The strength of his courage is what kept him safe in the lion's den.

Paul had it when he stood on the deck of a sinking ship and cried, "Be of good courage!" God required it of Joshua when He commanded him, "Be of good courage."

Stephen had it in his confrontation with the religious leaders of his day. As the Pharisees were throwing stones at him, his faith and courage so pleased God that he was able to see into heaven where the Lord was waiting for him.

Moral courage separates the men from the boys.

It's what makes some men successful, while those without it fail.

It takes courage to be a man of God.

Gideon was a young man when God chose him to be a leader.

He could hardly believe it.

His shyness and lack of self-confidence caused him problems.

God told him what to do, but he wasn't sure he could do it, or that it was from God. He had to have supernatural signs from God. He had to overhear men talking about him. He had to have all sorts of evidence that God favored him. But it all developed into courage in him and added to his faith.

Boldness is a form of courage.

Gideon needed that boldness.

When he added the courage of boldness to his faith, his actions brought victory to God's people and defeat to their enemies.

When you keep quiet before ungodly men, you give them the advantage. But when you speak up for Jesus, you give yourself and the Lord the advantage.

The fear of man is a form of moral cowardice. No wonder the Bible says not to fear what men can do to you.

Take a look at successful men in this world.

Without exception, they are bold in their identification with their belief, product or activity. They had to overcome their fear of men just like everybody else. But when they did and became bold in their confession, they became overcomers.

The pattern is basically Biblical and godly, but it is true even when used by the enemy.

Satan is the great counterfeiter, an archangel who can even now transform himself into an angel of light, who has taken God's patterns and twisted them to achieve his own perverted aims.

Communism, Nazism and other satanic political forces have used the pattern of identification to achieve their purposes.

Today in America, homosexuality successfully has used it.

When homosexuals "came out of the closet" and became bold in their identification with their homosexuality, when they overcame their fear of men and in their boldness openly confessed what they were (and sometimes flaunted it), they overcame much of society's stigma and changed people's attitudes.

The pattern was taken directly from the Bible and the teaching of our Lord.

Jesus said, "Except you lose your life for my sake and the gospel, you will not find it." He did not mean to opt for suicide or martyrdom to lose your life.

You lose it in identification with Him.

When we are willing to overcome our fear of men, openly identify with Jesus, and be bold in our confession of Him, we become overcomers.

Overcomers are spiritual achievers.

Billy Graham is an example. What do you think of when you hear his name? Christianity and a lot more.

While still in his teens, Billy walked an aisle after an evangelistic meeting with Mordecai Ham and made a total commitment to the Lord. In his early twenties he was preaching outdoors when William Randolph Hearst wrote a cryptic note to his newspaper editors in Los Angeles. It said, "Puff Graham."

Daily, Billy Graham was in the headlines. Soon, everywhere he went people recognized him as the young man who was preaching about Jesus Christ. Anything he had been prior to that time was gone, as he became totally identified with Jesus Christ.

Since then, his name has become a household word in homes around the world. And everywhere people associate him with Jesus Christ.

He lost his life in identification with Jesus Christ. Then he found a life he never would have known otherwise.

It's the same way with you.

You find it by losing it, and you lose it by trying to find it.

The choice is yours. The glory is God's.

*Life is composed of your choices and constructed by your words.**

Be bold both in word and deed.

Be the kind of whom it is said: "God was not ashamed to be called their God."

Hold to the courage of your convictions and learn to discriminate.

You need to be able to tell the difference between right and wrong, between the truth and a lie. "I would have you well versed and wise as to what is good, and innocent and guileless as to what is evil," is how Paul wrote it in his letter to the Romans.

Don't be moved by every person's personality, persuasion and belief. Learn to recognize what is right and stand on it.

"Stop listening to the teaching that contradicts what you know is right," say the Proverbs.

You need a godly pastor who can help you. He is to be your example in word, lifestyle, love, spirit, faith, purity . . .

And be real.

One of the common errors of men is to judge others by what they do, and themselves

---

*Ibid., p. 63.

by their intentions. Intentions are not actions. We are judged by what we do, not by what we intend to do.

Act with courage in the classroom, on the campus, at home and on the job.

Don't wait until your youth is gone to get the guts or wisdom to make your life count for God. Do it now!

I've tried to burn into men's hearts the need to read the Psalms and Proverbs to gain courage and wisdom. In addition to your regular Bible study, you need to read both books every day.

Start your day with a chapter from Proverbs, the book of wisdom. End your day with Psalms, the book of courage.

Don't allow yourself to develop bad thought patterns and habits that you'll have to undo and relearn later in life.

Lay the right foundation to your character. Be man enough and have the courage to begin right now, so you won't have to suffer all the remorse, regret and retribution later.

Don't waste your youth.

Let no man despise your youth.

Learn to say "no."

Identify yourself with Christ.

Reverence the right and reject the wrong.

Let your manhood be your glory.

Make it Christlike to begin with.

WIMPS: MADE IN AMERICA

3

WIMPS: MADE IN AMERICA

We were driving a van to Galveston for a men's meeting when Harold confessed that since he first made his decision to be a man of God, he had become confused. He wanted to be godly, but at the same time he wanted to be a success in business and reap the financial rewards.

How could he reconcile the two? How could he live wholeheartedly for God while his ego was driving him to become a financial success?

My answer was simple and pointed. "You don't kill your ego. You sanctify it.

"You don't make a success in life by concentrating on your weaknesses," I said. "You make a success by going to your strengths."

One of the things that religion has done is teach us to be in bondage to mediocrity, failure and poverty. Religion says it is a sin to achieve great things. Men all over the world are bound by that today, and as a consequence they are frustrated because the gifts, talents and attributes they have are buried in an effort to achieve spirituality.

"Don't kill your ego," I told Harold. "Sanctify it. Direct it. Channel it. Purify your motives and use your ego to achieve great things for God."

The only way Harold or any Christian man can be a success is to recognize his talents, gifts and abilities, and dedicate them to God so that God can maximize their potential.

The devil is a usurper. He'll steal everything he can from you. He'll usurp your character and personality, and put you into bondage if you allow him.

But God quickens you. He makes you alive. He plants creative ideas in your mind. He creates desires in your heart—not worldly ones, but godly ones. And then He fulfills His will by enabling you to realize those dreams.

The problem with many men is that they heard humility preached in the church, but saw inferiority practiced, and inferiority is what they learned. It's an error in understanding.

God created men to be successful—to be heroes and champions—and He placed that desire in every man's heart, in his ego. But men who base their lives on error will never fulfill that God-inspired goal for their lives.

My wife, Nancy, and I were sitting in a hotel restaurant in Tulsa. Our waitress was an attractive, vivacious young woman who stood out because of her poise and charm. With blond hair and honest blue eyes that sparkled while she talked, this 21-year-old looked like the All-American ideal.

When Nancy told her I was in town to speak to men and was the author of *Maximized Manhood,* her eyes narrowed. She looked at me flatly, intently, as if examining my qualifications for manhood. Seeming to satisfy herself, she spoke out softly with just a tinge of bitterness in her voice.

"Thank God," she said. "Thank God, someone is doing it. I get so tired of fighting them off, and trying to train them how to be men."

I was shocked to hear her, but I heard a lot more later.

This time Nancy and I were in San Jose, again in a hotel restaurant with a godly pastor, his wife and their two daughters. We were discussing the morning message I had preached which was directed at men.

I turned to the two lovely young women at the table and asked if they had received anything from the message.

"I think it is the most important ministry in the world," said the older of the two.

I asked why.

"Because I don't date anymore," she said.

"You what?" I was startled. "Why?"

"I don't date because most of the guys from church are one way at church and another way in the car. They're wimps!"

That was the first time I heard that accusation, but it wasn't to be the last. Just weeks later, another beautiful young woman told me she thought this ministry to men needed to go around the world—fast.

"I want a man," she stated. "I'm ready to get married, so I'm praying for God to send me a man. But so far, all I've found are wimps."

She was attractive, intelligent and feminine. Secure in her identity and femininity, she was available to make some man a wonderful life companion. But in her dating, her security was her undoing.

The men she dated seemed to be insecure in their manhood, inadequate in their ability to communicate, and intimidated by her security.

She admitted that in her dating she had tried to get down on the man's level, uncomfortable as it was, so she could be on a peer basis with him.

Another young woman felt she couldn't live up to her full potential because it alienated her from the men she knew. It isn't uncommon. I began to hear it more and more. Then I began to hear it from the men as well.

I was on a radio call-in talk show in Southern California which was popular among Christian young people. The subject of the program was men.

Most of the callers were women complaining about the same problems with their boyfriends, husbands and would-be husbands. But then a young man called to ask if I would answer a question about dating. I agreed.

"Mr. Cole, my question is this: When I take a girl out to dinner, should I offer to pay for her dinner or just let her pay for her own without asking?"

I let the program host answer it because I knew if I opened my mouth I'd give him a one-word answer: "Wimp!"

Men have become afraid and intimidated by secure and successful women. They are indecisive in their actions and, in their indecisiveness, have become weak. Hundreds of articles have been written about the "gender gap," but few offer any real solutions.

In one article I read recently, the columnist asked a successful woman friend which country she thought had the weakest men.

"I am sure in America we have more wimps per capita than any other country," she answered, "*especially among the younger men*. Most of the men I meet are wimps."

The columnist challenged her, saying it was the fault of the American woman who demanded that men cry, show their emotions and give up John Wayne for Alan Alda. Her answer: "That may be true. But they didn't have to make it so easy."

Psychologist Dan Kiley has risen to quick popularity by writing the book identifying the *Peter Pan Syndrome*. It's about men who never grow up.

The bottom line is this: Women still want a man who can accept responsibility, is chivalrous, makes decisions, shows courtesy and is kind. "Kindness makes a man attractive," Proverbs 19:22 says.

To be spiritual you don't have to die to your ego. And to be a man you don't have to die to your masculinity.

God created you in His image and for His glory. In that same verse it says He created woman for the man's glory. (1 Cor. 11:7.)

But how can a woman be the glory of the man unless that man is becoming the glory of God by being conformed to the image of Christ?

The problem is that many men are confused about what image they are to live up to. The image of Christ is your standard.

God calls each of us to live up to our own potential.

"To him that knoweth to do right and doeth it not, to him it is sin," the scripture reads.

If you know you are supposed to develop your potential, maximize your gifts, sanctify your ego in order to achieve—and you don't do it, then you are missing the mark God has for you.

You need to live for God-given dreams, divinely inspired desires, but die to the pride, fear and vain things of the world and the flesh.

The Bible teaches to die daily to those things, but it does not teach you to live a crucified life. It teaches you to live a resurrected life—a life lived in the power and glory that is within you according to Ephesians 3:20.

Once you crucify the fleshly things about you, get down off the cross! Jesus did!

Live!

Be all the man God wants you to be—doctor, lawyer, gas station attendant, missionary, pastor, legislator, zoo keeper or whatever. Determine to live up to the potential that is within you, placed there by God.

Don't be a wimp.

God needs men. Women need men. The world needs men.

Promotion doesn't come from the east or west—but from God. A man's gifts will make a way for him.

The reason we have a wimp problem today is because so many men have compromised their manhood.

God didn't call men to be trucemakers, but peacemakers. And peace only comes through victory.

In World War II, America fought a war until all her enemies were defeated. Whether in Africa, Europe or Asia, they were conquered. Peace resulted.

But in Vietnam we declared a truce. Our men in the armed forces came home feeling disgraced, and our country was miserable for years.

Soldiers want to fight through to victory. Politicians want to declare a truce.

Politicians do everything based on compromise. Soldiers in war don't want compromise, they want victory.

As it is in the natural, so it is in the spiritual.

Men who compromise—who settle for a truce with their sins—live in misery. Only when they fight through to victory do they live in peace.

Jesus did not declare a truce with Satan. The devil tried to reach a compromise with Him on the Mount of Temptation, but Jesus knew the only way He could give peace was by fighting for total victory. That's why the Word says it is a peace that surpasses the understanding of the world.

God doesn't want you to make a truce with your sin, but to fight until you have victory over it. Then you can live in peace.

Learn this now. Don't waste your youth, *learn now.*

Why live most of your life in misery when you can have peace and joy from this moment on?

When you read about the nation of Israel in Joshua, the ninth chapter, you find they were deceived into making a truce with their enemies. They did it because they didn't seek the counsel of God.

You're not too young to pray.

You're not too young to hear from God.

Samuel heard God's voice when he was only a child.

Hearing from God doesn't depend on age, but on relationship.

Establish your relationship with God now.

Don't waste your youth.

Prayer is the place of exchange between you and God. It is where you tell God all that is in your heart, and He puts in you what is in His heart.

Wishing will never be a substitute for prayer.

Truces are never a substitute for victory.

But men try those things because we live in a substitute society. We use weak substitutes out of habit. But can a weak, bland, insipid, tepid religion win a contest against the dynamic charisma of today's movies, music and pornographic eroticism?

Manners and culture are no substitute for the primitive power of God's presence. Don't be deceived.

Yet men try to substitute status symbols for the fruit of the Spirit.

Fantasy for reality.

Respectability for righteousness.

Works for faith.

Softness for gentleness.

Soft men can't take rough times. They capitulate. They make truces. God never told us to capitulate to our enemies. He told us to love them. And He told us to be victorious.

Jesus was a gentle man, but He was not a soft man. He taught a ruthlessness that is required by God. He said if your hand offends you, cut it off. He means that when you are tempted to do what is not right, have the ruthlessness and self-discipline to get away from it.

Men who are not ruthless with their own sins or with themselves are miserable. They make a truce with sex sins, alcohol, pornography, cheating, lying, masturbation, pride and lust. Then they try to escape from their misery through the very things that are making them miserable.

Dumb!

Jesus said, "Whatever offends you, CUT IT OFF!"

Wimps are afraid they might get hurt.

They avoid pain, not realizing the Biblical principle that even the world recognizes:

No gain without pain.

The reason you don't have victory is because you settle for a truce.

The reason you don't have more is because you settle for less.

Joseph, David, Samuel, Samson, Daniel—all were young men when they made their mark for God.

You can add your name to that list. You too can accomplish great things.

I don't know how old you are now, but think about this:

By the time you were 5 you already had received two-thirds of your lifetime impressions. By the time you were 7 you had two-thirds of your basic lifetime knowledge.

How old are you now?

You don't have another day to waste before you put to use all you have already gained.

Today is your "Day One."

SEX

4
SEX

So many people are startled when they hear or see the word "sex" in the Christian world. But why?

God made sex good.

Everything God makes, He makes perfect.

It is sin that blights what God creates.

It is sinful man that perverts sex.

God made sex good so that men would desire it and thus fulfill God's command to replenish the earth. In fact, God made sexual energy the power that holds the family together.

Sex is the physical union which symbolizes the spiritual union of man and woman. God created sex so a man and woman in the union of marriage could give themselves unreservedly to each other for mutual benefit and blessing.

God's prohibition of sex outside marriage was to protect sex from the very error we see as a result of immorality today. Venereal disease, emotional distress, abortion, divorce, and all forms of molestation and rape, even with children.

A woman was not made to be the object of man's lust, the prey of his predatory practices, at whose expense he gratifies himself.

Neither was she created to be the source of his downfall. It is a glory for a woman to help a man fulfill his manhood but a disgrace to be the means of his separation from God and his ruin.

God's Word is filled with warnings to young men concerning their unbridled passion, women's seducing flirtations and the result of allowing either to ruin them.

Street language has a brutal way of saying it, and it simply means that a penis has no conscience.

Conscience is programmed like a computer.

Garbage in, garbage out.

That's why God gave us His Word. It washes our minds and programs our consciences to righteousness.

The Bible says in Romans, chapter 1, that some people changed the truth of God into a lie, and made their image of God like corruptible man. Rather than submitting to the truth of the glorious and majestic Lord, they attempted to fashion Him into an image of themselves.

No wonder the scripture says those who did such things went on to other kinds of perversions. Peter preached on the Day of Pentecost, "Save yourself from this untoward (perverted) world."

The first symptom of error is taking scriptures and making them conform to your lifestyle, instead of taking your lifestyle and making it conform to the Word of God.

While I was in the San Francisco Bay area, a homosexual man attempted to justify himself to me by using the passage of scripture that says, "David and Jonathan had a love for each other that passed the love of women." Citing that, he justified his lusts for other men.

Perversion of life leads to perversion of scripture.

How inconsistent for homosexuals to contend that they can be "born-again Christians" and remain homosexual, while those who are heterosexual must repent of their adultery and forsake it.

Homosexuals call themselves "gay," but the fierceness of their spirit is being felt everywhere in the world today—even among young men in the Church.

I was at the headquarters of a national ministry recently when one of the young men on staff asked me for some counsel and prayer. He had read one of my books and believed I could help him.

He confessed that while watching the Olympics during the summer he had experienced an erotic stir for a swimmer shown on television.

I told him that his desire was very probable for a young man because of the way some of the young ladies looked in their bathing suits. But he was right to be concerned, because his reply shocked me.

"It was the men, not the women, that tempted me."

In recent days I have heard of a Bible college president who had to resign because of homosexuality, a pastor openly admitting it at the time of his resignation, a youth pastor confessing that his desire for ministry was a cover to meet young men, and young men in a church group experimenting with it.

Gay rights activists are trying to get government to prevent discrimination. They follow that up by petitioning the educational system to allow homosexuality to be taught in the classroom as an acceptable "alternative" lifestyle.

A pervasive perversion of morals is rampant.

In Melbourne, Australia, as I left the building after a men's meeting, a young man stopped me to challenge the teaching.

"Do you mean to tell me that as a single man I'm supposed to live without sex?" He asked it brazenly, obviously wanting to contest me in order to justify his promiscuity.

"Do you believe the Bible?" I asked mildly.

"I do," he said.

"The Bible says that fornication is a sin, and that outside of marriage sex is not to be indulged in," I said.

He countered me, "That was meant for centuries ago when the standards of behavior were different."

"Don't you believe in personal salvation?" I asked.

"Yes, but the way to live it has changed," was his excuse.

"Sir," I said, "the Bible and its standards have never changed. You obviously want to adhere only to portions of scripture that suit you, but you are not interested in truly submitting yourself to righteousness. You are like those whom Jesus rebuked when He said they could justify their every inconsistency. Don't argue with me."

With that rebuke I walked away. He could take it and make the most of his salvation, or leave it and see the resulting misery in his life.

God never gave His Word so that we could take portions of it and justify our lifestyle. That is the symptom of cultism. God requires us to take our lives and make them conform to His Word.

We submit to the image and will of God, not make God into our image according to our will.

God's Word is the source of your faith and the sole rule of your conduct.

You cannot read pornographic materials and attend porn films without being affected by the unclean spirits that produced them.

Pornography will pollute, contaminate and infect both your mind and spirit. With the pollution comes confusion that results in inconsistency of life, mental blight, spiritual weakness and separation from fellowship with God.

You cannot live that way and have power from God.

God's power is released to the degree that obedience is exercised, and no more.

All God's promises are conditional. His love is not conditional, His promises are.

"To him that knoweth to do good, and doeth it not, to him it is sin," and "Whatsoever is not of faith is sin" is what the Word says.

The restraint of the Holy Spirit is there to keep you pure before God in thought, word and deed.

Puberty is always full of problems. So many changes take place.

The discovery of virility in manhood often brings experimentation with masturbation. However, the development of habitual masturbation can affect a man during his entire life. Whether single or married, it can have harmful effects.

No matter what any psychologist says or how any popular author attempts to justify it, explain away guilt or give assurances, there is still a basic wrong to it. Perhaps not physiologically, as some old wives' tales say, but at least psychologically.

Most men cannot masturbate without fantasizing. That is what pornography is all about, creating fantasies in your mind. Fantasies are your creation of an erotic act that only can be satisfied with someone else or by masturbation.

All pornography is idolatrous.

The image is created in your mind. It is actually an idol and makes the act of habitual masturbation become an act of worshipping that idol.

In turn, it creates a stronghold in your mind and a snare to your life.

Some people think I'm crazy for preaching this right from the pulpit, but I encounter men all the time who have lost all sense of balance because of habitual masturbation. One man asked, "How many times a day would you consider habitual?" That's reason enough to preach it!

The idolatrous fantasizing and private sexual sins are actually sins against your own manhood. God hates cheating of every kind. "Cheaters never prosper" is what the children cry, and it is the truth. "He that covereth his sins shall never prosper" is how the Bible puts it.

This is not because an angry god will openly expose your sins, but because the effects of them will show eventually in your lack of productivity and the mental and physical drain that becomes evident to those around you. Sometimes, though, you go too far and expose your own sins. That's what happened to Keith, who wrote me the following letter:

"I am a born-again Christian who this evening sat down to listen to your 'Straight Talk: X-Rated' tape series. One particular thing you said about sexual sin really hit home; that is to 'deal with that sin at the altar now—rather than let it be exposed later, in the open.' Well, I didn't deal with my sexual sin when I heard you speak a year or so ago and now my sin has been exposed.

"I am an Army man with eight years in the service, married to a wonderful Christian woman. I am presently accused of child molestation. The accusation is true, and I face possible court martial and the loss of my wife, as well as my military career.

"Had I made that trip to the altar and really given this sin to God, I would not be going through such an experience today. I believe God gave me the opportunity to repent before Him and turn from sexual sin. Because I didn't turn to Him then, I must turn to Him now for mercy and grace with the outcome.

"I share these things with you so that other men can be spared the experience I am now going through. I know God is merciful and will see me through, but the cost is so great. Please pray for me. God bless your ministry. It is seriously needed."

Keith is just one of many who lost everything because he didn't have the courage to walk down an aisle and admit he needed God. He didn't have to lose everything, though.

You don't have to face what Keith is facing today, either. Fill your mind with the Word *now*, program your conscience with it *now*, and don't let the perversion of the world affect you.

Experimentation is the rule of adolescence. God has placed a desire in your heart for adventure so that someday you will be ready to live as a man on your own.

But experimentation becomes perverted in the world and twisted into "try everything once."

It is especially true on college campuses.

Experimentation is also the means by which the conscience is crossed to allow for any type of behavior.

Sin always promises to please and serve, but in reality it always enslaves and dominates.

Marijuana promises to please and serve. So does alcohol, cocaine and pornography. Ask the addict. Look at the enslavement he suffers.

Yoked to heroin, stealing to satisfy his craving, losing all morals and eventually all self-respect, finally there is nothing to restrain him from doing evil. It didn't start that way, but it ended that way.

No wonder Jesus says, "My yoke is easy and my burden is light."

It gives you an easy feeling when you don't have sin in your life.

It makes you lighthearted when you are not burdened with guilt.

There is no burden to telling the truth, living honestly, loving others and serving God. Being yoked to righteousness is a joy forever.

Program your conscience to righteousness by the Word of God.

Learn it.

Get it into your spirit.

Live it.

Even in the Church there has crept in a false philosophy based on a devilish half-truth. By quoting, "There is no condemnation to them which are in Christ Jesus," some are deceived into thinking they can party, get drunk, fornicate or indulge in anything else in "moderation" and still be a man of God.

Untrue.

That entire verse of the Bible says, "There is now no condemnation to them which are in Christ Jesus, *which walk not after the flesh but after the Spirit.*"

Jim was a young man who had a desire to be an evangelist. He desired to be someone whom others would look up to, and he had some talent for it as well. But he reminded me of what my friend, Jack Mackey, once said:

"Illusions of grandeur are not visions of greatness."

Fact and fantasy are not compatible.

Jim saw himself as a popular young man with a keen desire to accomplish great things for God, but others saw him as an inconsistent young man who, from day to day, was a constant drain on the ministry and minister alike.

He wasn't teachable.

Oh, he heard the Word, but he wasn't a doer of the Word.

Jim couldn't overcome his own lusts. Periodic bouts with porno films, magazines and cable movies caused mental dullness that resulted in his inconsistencies.

"He that ruleth his spirit is better than he that taketh a city," Proverbs says.

True.

One of the first questions I ask when people tell me about a guy whose behavior is inconsistent and radically altered is, "Is it a woman or pornography?"

Sin always alters behavior.

It has since the Garden of Eden when it began with Adam.

Keeping yourself free from sin allows God's glory and power to flow through your life.

Do you read the Bible? Apply it to your life.

"Thy Word have I hid in my heart that I might not sin against Thee," is how it's written in the Psalms.

Love God's Word.

Apply it to your life.

You're never too young.

But someday you may be too old.

HOW DO YOU SPELL "RELEASE"?

5
HOW DO YOU SPELL "RELEASE"?

We were in a rustic Colorado lodge, miles from the nearest city, to start a men's retreat on the opening day of deer season. About a hundred men from Amarillo, Texas, joined in an opening chorus which sounded like an anthem, as our male voices reverberated in our ears and drifted out into the woods. God heard our songs of praise and met us that night in a way we would never forget.

It is a rare occasion when you see a large crowd of men completely lose their defenses and become real with each other and with the Lord. But it happened that night when they heard the principle of "release" from

John, chapter 20, and forgave sins that many of them had been carrying their entire lives. One man's testimony had such an impact on each of us that it bears repeating a thousand times.

He was big and rough. His face looked like a road map to every honky-tonk in Texas. But he stood there in tears and told us about the release he had just experienced.

"For years I have wanted to live my life for God," he said. "I have always wanted to be admired and respected, a man who could even love himself. But instead, my life has been up and down, on and off, to the point that at times I have just cried out to God and asked Him to please, please relieve me and help me to walk that straight and narrow path. But I kept doing the same old things. I hated myself for what I did to my wife, my kids, my friends, yet I couldn't seem to stop. That is—until tonight. I don't know how to describe it, but right now I *know* I'm a new man.

"See, it wasn't until tonight that I understood about forgiveness and that I could hold someone else's sins in me. When I heard that if we don't forgive our parents for their sins, then we retain them and keep them inside us, it hit me like a ton of bricks. That was *me*!

"I grew up in foster homes. My folks put me out when I was 2 years old. They lived in the same town, and I knew of them, but I never met my mother until I was older.

"My dad, he was a tough old drunk, hated by everyone in town. Because they knew I was his son, they hated me, too. I had to fight my way through school. It seemed like everyone was against me. I hated my dad so much that when he died I went to the funeral just so I could spit in his face in the coffin.

"When I was 16, my best friend kept bragging about some woman he was dating who was great in bed. When he brought her around to show off to me, I recognized her as my mother. I hated her for it.

"But tonight, when I heard what Jesus said about forgiveness, I realized for the first time that the reason I was so messed up is because I never forgave my mom and dad. I hated them and held on to that hatred of their sins, but it bound those sins to my life. I ended up doing the same things I hated them for.

"But I prayed that prayer tonight and forgave them. I really meant it, too, because I needed to get it out of me. I'm telling you, I feel like 10 tons came off me. Right now I'm a new man. *Jesus just made me a new man*!"

Every man in the room was in tears by the time he finished. They broke out in applause to express their gratitude to the Lord for the miracle. Many of them testified that they also had incredible experiences of release. Quite a night.

Men need to understand that principle.

You need to learn it now—get hold of it—and let the constant application of its truth keep you free.

Jesus said, "Receive the Holy Spirit. If you forgive the sins of anyone, they are forgiven. If you retain the sins of anyone, they are retained."

In other words, admit the Holy Spirit into your life. Now—having received the Holy Spirit and being guided and directed by Him—the sins you forgive are released, and the sins you don't forgive are retained in your life.

If you forgive, you release. By not forgiving, you retain. So simple. So profound. So divine. So true.

A young minister had his life changed when he acted in faith on that same principle.

As a young man, Dwayne had seen his father commit adultery in his parents' bedroom. The sight and sound of that stamped itself on his mind and lodged in his spirit.

Growing into manhood, Dwayne constantly battled a spirit of lust, fantasies and fornication. Now that he was married, he battled thoughts of adultery.

But when he heard the truth of the principle of release and forgave his father, his life completely changed. Dwayne has been free ever since from every thought, image and desire that had plagued him for so long.

I just finished a phone conversation with Bob Rogers, the director of the Teen Challenge rehabilitation centers in Southern California. Bob had brought all the men from every center in the area to a meeting to hear the principle of release.

Most of them were from the streets, former drug addicts, many with arrest records, some fresh out of prison. Street people who are toughened by mistrust have learned not to share their personal feelings with others. They keep their true emotions inside and their past lives a secret. They live by their wits; think fast on their feet; learn to lie, cheat, manipulate; and con their way into and out of situations.

The staff at the centers constantly battles skepticism regarding the men they counsel because they are never sure when they are hearing the truth. Men walk forward to pray oftentimes just to gain approval from their counselor, instead of with a sincere heart to seek God.

But Bob told me the staff is still feeling the impact of what happened at that meeting. The men stood up after their prayer of release and openly told the most intimate, private statements of truth about their past lives and what had just happened to them as they prayed the prayer.

One man had been in six drug rehabilitation programs, gone through hospital and prison counseling, and was none the better for it. But that day he forgave his father for molesting him, for beating his mother and for offending his sisters. He said that for the first time in his life he felt free from the bitterness, bondage and perverseness unforgiveness had caused in his life.

Then a young man in the front row stood up to tell the crowd that he had just forgiven his father for abandoning the family. But more difficult for him was to forgive his brother who had beaten him, violated his sisters and insulted his mother. He said the hatred for his brother was so intense, he could use it as a tool. When he turned it loose, it released such a fury inside him that he could kill six men at once. I don't know if that was why he served his prison sentence, but as release from that hatred boiled up and out of him, he stood there in front of everyone weeping, head bowed, broken in spirit, never to be the same again.

I stepped forward, put my arms around him, and with his head held to my shoulder, said, "I want you to feel a father's arms and know what it is to have a father's love." For him it was like a knot of bitterness inside had been untied that day, giving him the freedom to be his own man.

Another stood to say he forgave his father for committing adultery while his mother lay dying of cancer. The father had remarried three weeks after she died, and then committed adultery again within the first week of his new marriage.

I looked over the group of 150 men and asked a simple question.

"How many of you feel that your father is mainly responsible for the problems you've had in your life?"

Almost to a man, their hands went up. It was dramatic evidence of the importance of the father-son relationship. It made painfully clear why God's Word says so much about fathers and sons and the duty of fathers to teach their sons righteous living.

But how incredible, how miraculous, the healing that occurs when by faith, men act on the principle of release and experience total freedom for the first time. Only after they are released are they free to become the man God wants them to be.

Men must accept responsibility for their lives.

Your refusal to accept that responsibility, or to relieve yourself of it by blaming someone else, will block your maturity.

Maturity doesn't come with age; it comes with the acceptance of responsibility.

You cannot mature if you go through life blaming parents, friends, relatives, education (or lack of it), environment or heredity for your immaturity.

You alone are responsible for your life.

Tom is a young man who had all kinds of problems while growing up. His dad was a religious man who went to church every time the doors were open and faithfully gave the church his time and money.

His dad never had time for Tom, though. He was too busy with church. Elders' meetings, choir rehearsals, Sunday school meetings, maintenance of the grounds, bus driving, anything and everything the pastor mentioned that needed to be done took most of the dad's free time.

Work took the rest of it. The store he owned needed him every day from 8 to 5, and sometimes he worked overtime to order goods, pay bills, stock shelves, clean floors and keep up a good business.

Too busy for Tom.

Tom grew up religious, but in his heart he resented God and disliked Jesus. To Tom, Jesus took all his dad's time.

Tom's dad would talk at home about how he was helping with the financial needs of the church; but when Tom wanted to go on a youth outing, his dad refused, saying they didn't have the money.

The hostility Tom built up toward his father and God transferred itself into negative attitudes toward family, relatives, teachers, bosses, even friends. Throughout his early life, that basic conflict disturbed Tom.

Even when he heard the truth later, it was hard for Tom to receive it and act on it. Over the years the hostility had hardened his heart so that it was very difficult for him to forgive his dad. Finally, he did. It was slow in coming, with forgiveness for an injustice one week, then forgiveness for something else weeks later.

Tom is a whole man today because of that release. But his dad never changed. He still puts all his efforts into his religion while neglecting his family.

Wasted manhood.

Religion can be awfully hard.

That's why *Christianity is not "religion," it is relationship.*

To honor your mother and father is the first commandment with promise. The promise is long life.

The Word talks about fathers and sons in various ways:

"God puts out the lights of the man who curses his father or mother . . .

"It is a wonderful heritage to have an honest father . . .

"An old man's grandchildren are his crowning glory. A child's glory is his father . . .

"A rebellious son is a calamity to his father . . .

"Reverence for God gives a man deep strength.

His children have a place of refuge and strength."

The Word also says fathers are blessed when they raise their children in the nurture and admonition of the Lord. But if they don't, it becomes a curse.

Equally emphatic is the admonition to young men to honor their fathers in the Lord, and that to rebel is to invite calamity.

Where a father is sinful, in error, partial, unfair, mistaken, ungodly or in outright rebellion against God, it is simply dumb for you as a young man to allow *his* sins to ruin *your* life!

You are to love your father, honor him and submit to his authority *in the Lord.* It does make a difference.

Make sure your own heart is clean before God concerning your father. Where your father has made a mistake, forgive him so you don't retain it and pass it down someday to your own children.

The principle of release is vital to you right now. It will keep you free from other people's sins all your life. It will help you mature and move from one stage of development to another.

There are really only two things you do in life:

Enter and leave.

How you leave determines how you enter.

How you leave your mother's womb determines how you will enter infancy. Then you leave infancy for childhood, childhood for adolescence, and on it goes through each stage of life and every change you make.

When you leave home—to work, marry, go to school, join the army, or for any other reason—you cannot carry resentments, bitterness, hatred, loneliness, inferiority or any other excess baggage. If you carry it with you, you will be stuck with it in the next stage, situation or relationship you enter.

Each leaving and entering process creates crises in our lives. The crisis of change is normal to life. Any crisis you go through will have sorrow in it. But sorrow is life's greatest teacher, if you don't waste it.

All true joy is born out of sorrow.

You only know the joy of graduation if you have first known the sorrow of study and homework. You only know the joy of salvation after you experience the godly sorrow for your sins which leads to repentance.

Don't let your crises separate you from God. Use them to bring you closer to Him. Release the sins of those you are leaving behind. Let God take you through the crisis to the next stage.

God wants every change in your life to be good. God is *for* you, not *against* you.

Perhaps your father raised you in church and never sinned against you, your family or others. But if you have any bitterness, envy, hurt, resentment or other such feeling toward anyone—someone at school who insulted you, a girl who made fun of you, a teacher who demeaned you, a relative who slighted you, a mother who ridiculed you, release them. FORGIVE!

Don't bear other people's sins. Release them from your life as Jesus taught you.

Each of the men I told you about had problems for years in their lives because they carried the sins of their fathers with them as they grew up. Not until after they had been hurt and suffered so much did they realize what had happened to them.

But you can do what Jesus said to do.

By faith, receive God's Spirit and power in your life and forgive your father and others, so you can release sins and not retain them for your own hurt.

Pray this prayer right now:

God, by faith and in accordance with Your Word, I receive Your Holy Spirit power into my life. By the ability of Your Spirit and through the authority of Your Word, I forgive my father his sins against me. All of them. I release them out of my life. I don't want to bear his sins any longer.

I want to be free from everyone's sins, so I forgive everybody. Make me free, Lord, to be the man You want me to be. Thank You.

Don't waste your youth on someone else's sins.

Be your own man.

Love your dad. If you have further hurt or bitterness, repeat the prayer again.

If you can, talk to your father about it.

Get the release for both of you.

How do you spell release?

F-O-R-G-I-V-E-N-E-S-S.

THE INVISIBLE MAN

6
THE INVISIBLE MAN

A plane crashes into the Potomac. Rescue workers race to save the drowning victims, but one woman cannot be reached. A bystander throws off his jacket and jumps into the icy river to save her. The next day he is heralded across the country as a hero.

When asked later what motivated his act of bravery, he simply said that at the spur of the moment he saw a need and knew he had to help.

Courage means acting on a need greater than self. But there are really no spur-of-the-moment decisions.

Every decision a man makes is based on a lifetime of decisions which either enhanced or diminished his character.

Character is not the same as personality. Personality is seen in public; character is built by what you do in private. There are "has beens" in every area of life—music, movies, television, sports, church. They built their personalities, but neglected their character.

When the personality wears off, only the character remains.

A man who has learned to honor God privately will show good character in his decisions publicly.

You honor God by believing His Word. You dishonor Him through unbelief.

You honor God by trusting in Jesus. You dishonor Him by rejecting the Savior.

You honor God through obedience to His Word. You dishonor Him by ignoring or disobeying it.

God honors those who honor Him.

The story of Mordecai and Haman in the Book of Esther shows it so clearly. These are not Bible fairy tales, but real instances in the lives of real men.

Mordecai honored God in his thoughts, words, motives and deeds. Because of the character it built, in a moment of need he was able to protect the king from harm, and the king decided to honor him for it.

Haman was the king's right-hand man, a public man with personality plus. He hated Mordecai. Haman conspired to do away with Mordecai and all the others who served his God. When the king asked what to do to honor the man who had served the crown so nobly, Haman thought it was meant for him and gave the king a grand idea to be honored before the entire country.

As it turned out, Mordecai received the honors, while Mr. Personality was hanged on the gallows he had built for Mordecai.

God honors those who honor Him.

You don't play around with God. God is for real.

Sunday school students know about the three Hebrew children who were sentenced to death in a fiery furnace, but the Lord Himself appeared in the furnace with them. They came out alive without even the smell of smoke. They had been sentenced to death because they believed the honor of God was more important than their own lives.

Some things in life are more important than life itself.

The Hebrew children had built into their characters the honor of God, and God honored them by saving their lives.

The battle Joseph fought was when he was all alone with Potiphar's wife. He could have "gotten away" with sin, but he understood that the honor of God was more important than his own youthful lusts.

His reason for running from her seductions was clear. "How can I do this great wickedness and sin against God?" he asked. His identification with God was real and true. He wasn't concerned about himself, but about the honor of God.

God honored him in return by promoting him to the highest government position in a country where he was an alien. Later, Joseph was able to save his entire family. He lived the balance of his life in complete luxury because he learned in his youth that the honor of God was more important than any selfish desires he had. He knew if he honored God, God would honor him. And He did.

Instead of being the victim of sin, Joseph was a victor.

There is a world of difference between "maximized" manhood and "victimized" manhood.

Remember Keith who didn't cleanse his spirit of sexual sins when he had the opportunity and found dishonor as a result of not honoring God? He thought it too embarrassing to honor God by repentance, and now is being embarrassed for life before the whole world with his dishonorable discharge. He was dishonored by man, instead of honored by God.

Sin is always a form of insanity.

It is dumb.

Esau was like that in the Book of Genesis. He sold his birthright to his brother for a bowl of soup. He traded away his God-given eternal rights for a bowl of soup that only lasted a moment.

The other night I met an anguished young man. He wanted to serve God, but under great pressure he violated his conscience and had sex with a young woman. Even while doing it, he knew it was wrong. Though angry with himself for trading away his virtue and the honor of God, he had his moment of guilt-ridden pleasure. Now he faces a lifetime of horror from herpes.

It is honoring to God and to your manhood when you don't succumb to temptation. When Jesus overcame temptation, He "returned in the power of the Spirit." When you honor God, you strengthen your character, increase the stature of your manhood and find favor with God and man.

Jeb Magruder was involved in the Watergate scandal that rocked our country in the 70s. He since has repented and gone on to work in the ministry, but he knows about the evils of self-interest, pride and arrogance. Speaking from first-hand experience, Jeb tells of what happened in the Watergate fiasco:

"We were willing to subvert our own moral character to the character of the group, and we went down the tubes in the process," he writes. "There were 38 people involved in Watergate, and most of them were very competent, well-to-do lawyers and businessmen, and all with good motives. We didn't come to Washington to commit crimes, but we did."

God deals with us according to His Word, not according to our society's norm. Just because others do it is not a reason for us to do it. Our standard is obedience to the Word of God, and that is what we will be judged by when we stand before God.

We will all stand before God one day.

Consider Eli.

He was a priest in Israel, judging the nation and leading the people in worship. His sons lived a life contrary to the will of God, and the Bible says, "They made themselves vile."

In their immorality, cheating God's people, lying to their father and indulging in sensual pleasures, they showed their rebellion to God. Their behavior showed they despised God's Word. Sure they had heard it—but they didn't live it.

The prophet Samuel warned Eli about what God thought of their dishonor to Him, and exactly what he said came true. Eli died and all his sons were killed.

The reason: Eli honored his sons above God. When they made themselves vile, he dishonored God by not restraining them. God required Eli to restrain his sons to preserve the honor of God, but when Eli didn't do it, he lost everything.

The honor of God is the criterion for our way of living.

There is nothing more important than the honor of God.

When there is no fear of the Lord in the heart of the Church, there is no restraint in our society from doing evil. Running with the crowd instead of leaving it for the honor of God is costly.

"Can a man take fire to his bosom and not be burned?" the Bible says.

A Seattle newspaper reported the following that illustrates the point:

"It all started as a teenage obsession with the game Dungeons and Dragons and evolved into the worship of the devil. Then the youth began to beat his mother and threaten her with curses. The woman has spent long nights of worry when she knew her son was at satanic ceremonies.

"The 'boy' in his mid-to-late teens has become uncontrollable and threatens to kill her or cast evil spells on her. A priest agreed to discuss the subject only if his name was not used.

"He said that since the mid-1960s, the church has become skeptical of the existence of the devil as a personal being, and there is a growing belief that evil exists almost as an institution. The priest, who has studied pastoral psychology, said teenagers may accept the occult because they are not satisfied with the spiritual experience of the church and start looking for a different experience. That could mean drug abuse, promiscuous sexual experience or the occult."

There is a personal devil. God's Word tells us that Satan is the father, or originator, of all lies. Because of that, all sin is deceitful in its character.

That is why you need God's Word, which is Truth, and to have God's Spirit, the "Spirit of Truth." When God's Spirit is working in you, you will be guided into all truth.

Truth is basic to everything you are and everything you do. You must have truth so you can recognize lies and fight for the honor of God.

Honesty means being honorable in intention, thoughts and action. The core of integrity is honesty.

"The Lord hates cheating and delights in honesty," the Bible tells us.

Be honest with God. Even in prayer.

Prayer isn't just getting down on your knees, or bowing your head to mutter a few syllables of hope in order to satisfy the demand for religious exercise. True prayer is getting together with God to share your life and all that it holds, telling Him your concerns for yourself, your family, your friends, and sharing His concern for the world.

It's normal to pray.

Every man desires recognition, especially from someone in authority. In prayer, we find recognition, appreciation, acceptance and affection from God Himself.

The sin of omission is as great as the sin of commission. Neglecting to pray will separate you from God as much as giving in to temptation.

Finding friendship with God is life's greatest treasure. Being alone with God will rid you of loneliness.

Men who know how to pray exercise a boldness toward life that enables them to be more than conquerors. They know God is *for* them; they need not fear anyone who is *against* them.

The result of prayer in private will be a life of boldness and courage in public.

Prayer is an invisible tool which wields itself in the visible world.

The entire physical world is made up of tiny molecules that are invisible to the naked eye. Likewise, the natural world is made up of the elements of the supernatural world. That which is visible is created by that which is invisible.

Loving is invisible.

Giving is visible.

Honor is invisible.

Obedience is visible.

The degree of giving is the visible evidence of the degree of loving.

When the Israelites had their hearts pure before God in Exodus, chapter 35, they honored Him by eagerly giving their best.

But later Malachi had to tell them their hearts no longer honored God because they were now giving Him their weak and crippled animals for sacrifices.

How much money you give God in the visible world depends on how much you love God in the invisible world.

How you work in school, on the job and around the house reflects the obedience you have toward God in your heart.

Giving and obedience are two different things. It is wrong to exercise one and neglect the other.

You cannot gain by sacrifice what you lose through disobedience.

The honor of God in your life will result in both giving and obedience.

If you make a quality decision to honor God with your thoughts, words, motives and deeds, God will honor you.

We live in a world where men in communist countries and elsewhere are being imprisoned, shot, tortured and persecuted for their faith in Christ and their desire to honor God in a corrupt society. Men who are barely 12 years old refuse to give in to atheistic governmental policies. Men are hazarding their lives for Christ.

Then some simpering, silly, stupid guy thinks it's some kind of macho manhood to show off his sinful lusts to a crowd of church kids, and they all just stand there.

Where is the honor of God?

Do you feel pressured to go along with things like that? Do you feel peculiar because you don't laugh at it?

Dare to be different.

So many men today are like lukewarm celery. When celery is cut and heated in soup, it tastes great. When it's cold and fresh from the refrigerator, it's delicious. But when it's been laying around the sink for two days — limp, lukewarm and lifeless — it tastes terrible!

That's what today's androgynous man is like. Not knowing whether to be bold or backward, decisive or suppliant, lacking in the understanding of truth, without any sense of morality or the honor of God, he pours on a little hot, a little cold, and ends up lukewarm.

As one girl put it, "It's enough to make you puke!"

God must have felt the same way when He said in His Word He would spew the lukewarm people out of His mouth!

Today, acceptable forms of behavior include lying, cheating, stealing, bribery, immorality, even murder. Today the virgin, not the fornicator, is laughed at. The man who doesn't cheat in business is considered the odd ball.

But God says He "hates those who say that bad is good, and good is bad."

It is tough sometimes to side with God for righteousness. The man who wants to follow God's Word and not be a partaker of other men's sins, to keep himself pure and live a righteous life, will find acceptance with God but not always with peers.

Make the honor of God more important than the honor of your peers.

God will honor you openly.

God will pour out for you honors that you cannot achieve on your own — IF you consider His honor always more important than your own desires.

Think of the difference when you leave this life — the difference between an "honorable" or "dishonorable" discharge is the difference between Heaven and Hell.

WORKING HARD, GOING NOWHERE

7 WORKING HARD, GOING NOWHERE

Kevin was a young guy with a real heart for God.

He was leading witnessing teams, conducting prayer meetings and involving himself in activities to further the cause of Christ. In his city he was respected and appreciated by all who knew him.

Everyone admitted that he was one fine brother.

But his ministry never seemed to grow.

Finances and personnel were always a problem.

Personally, he was friendly and pleasant so that others were drawn to him, and he really took great joy in counseling, praying and helping others in whatever way he could. Yet, he never seemed to grow or go anywhere.

His problem was that he wanted authority but not accountability.

He could never bring himself to give an account to anyone for his actions, lifestyle or ministry. He had an excuse for every failure, then covered it up with a praise report of what had just happened in someone's life. The result was a no-growth situation.

Every man has to live with accountability.

The Apostle Paul wrote to Timothy and said there were six things for which he was accountable in his life:

- Reputation
- Ethics
- Morality
- Temperament
- Habits
- Maturity

God is concerned about these things in your life, so concerned that He wrote a book for you through men whose lives were in danger for writing it. The truth in the Bible will lead you to be accountable for each of those six things.

No man lives or dies unto himself.

Someone once said it this way, "To thine own self be true."

Truth is the bedrock of your integrity. Your personal integrity is the cornerstone of your character.

Truth is not an option in life.

The more you base your life on truth, the better will be your way and the greater will be your life.

The more you base your life on a lie, the harder will be your way and the less significant will be your life.

Truth eliminates guilt, fear and hiding. The truth alone can set you free.

Truth is without partiality.

Truth can never die.

Truth will stand the test of time.

Love truth. Men may know truth, recognize it, admit it, but not love it. To love truth is to make it part of your life. To have the benefits of truth you must first accept it into your life.

Truth, honesty, faith, love, humility, wisdom, courage — all are virtues of manhood.

Faithfulness is the cornerstone of success.

"Commit thou to faithful men *who shall be able*" is how the scripture reads. Faith comes before ability.

So much is being attempted in churches today by putting men who seem "able" into places of leadership. Then the whole church is frustrated because things go wrong. The Word tells us to make "faithful" men the leaders, and God will add the ability. Able men who are not faithful are a burden.

God commits to character, not talent.

John is a company president, godly in his conduct and faithful to his word, well-liked and well-respected by everyone in the company, yet few realize he started as a shipping clerk. He was faithful in shipping, and God made him able to be promoted into leadership.

Consistency, decisiveness and moral strength are other virtues of manhood.

Inconsistency is a mark of immaturity. It can take a heavy toll on you and others. Why wait until you have made mistakes and have to undo all the wrong? Learn to do it right now.

Don't waste your youth.

A man who wasted his youth and half his life wrote me the following letter:

"I was saved when I was 14 and am now 45 years old. All my life I have been afraid to stand up for Jesus, until your meeting last night, Mr. Cole. I started going to church a month ago — wanting to be close to God again. I have seen men all around me raising hands to God and praising Him, but I did not respond because in my heart I thought I'd look foolish. Last night I raised my hands to God. I knew then that it takes a real man to be open to God in front of others.

"I have worked hard all my life getting nowhere, neglecting my family and passing all the responsibilities of raising my children to my wife. One day I woke up — my children were grown and there was discord between the kids and my wife. My son was on drugs and stealing everything we own to support his habit.

"We went to psychiatrists instead of to God. In desperation, my son tried to take his life. God had to send someone else to do what I should have done — lead my son to the Lord. When my son was in jail, I asked others to pray for my son, but I did not pray myself.

"The whole tragedy of this is that I knew to go to God in prayer. I could have saved my son from the anguish of drugs, poor self-image and deep depression. I could have been prosperous instead of poor. I could have saved my wife the pressure of working to help out, while running the household, paying the bills and disciplining the children.

"Thanks to God and your ministry, my life has changed. Please use this letter for your ministry if you see fit."

Thirty years of suffering, sorrow and pain that could have been avoided.

That's why I'm writing to you about the virtues of manhood and telling you to apply God's Word to your life at 14 instead of waiting until you're 45 — then having to live with the past.

It takes time to be holy, wise and proficient.

It takes time to become Christlike in your manhood.

The thing that made America great is not the virtue of her wealth, but the wealth of her virtue. That's why we need to keep virtue in our country. That's why you need virtue in your life — the virtue of Christlikeness.

The hardest thing, it seems, for a man to do is to admit he's wrong. Men have a tough time with the willingness to correct their mistakes. But it's really the first step in manhood.

Take that step.

Then follow after right-ness with God.

You must be willing to change if you want to be mature. You must be willing to leave behind old friendships that keep you bound to the world. Remember, you must not allow yourself to partake of another man's sins. If you have friends who are dragging you down, leave them behind.

Likewise, God has made you a unique man with a unique pattern for your life. You cannot find your own pattern if you allow yourself to live by the patterns of others. Don't let others force you into their pattern. Learn from others, but seek God to find your own pattern.

The danger of following the crowd is that you don't know where they may take you, or what their motivations are. The three most powerful motivations in the world are:

- Hate
- Fear
- Greed

But God gives one more that is more powerful than all others:

- Love

Most of what is called "love" today is really just lust. You need to know the difference between them.

The distance between love and lust is as far as Heaven is from Hell.

The qualities of love are:

- Patience
- Kindness
- Generosity
- Humility
- Courtesy
- Unselfishness
- Good temperament
- Guilelessness
- Sincerity

Each of these is a virtue of manhood. That's why I have said around the world that true manhood and Christlikeness are synonymous.

It's true.

When the love of God is put into your heart and life by the Holy Spirit, those elements are what is produced in your life.

Love conquers hate, fear and greed.

Love is the toughest substance known to man.

God commands us to love. He rightfully commands love because love centers in the will. If you will to love, then you'll love. Turn your heart toward love. Rid yourself of every other motivation. Let love for God motivate your manhood just as it did Jesus when He was on earth in the form of a man.

Love.

Don't waste your youth.

Love now.

Be accountable for your actions.

Be faithful in all you do.

BEND, BOW OR BURN

8
BEND, BOW OR BURN

After Roy greeted me when I got off the plane in Louisville, I asked him, "How's it going?"

He looked at me quizzically and asked, "You haven't heard?"

"Heard what?" I asked.

"My son tried to commit suicide the other night, and I've spent a couple of long nights and tense days because of it."

"I'm sorry to hear that," I said. "Anything I can do to help?"

"Not right now," he said. "He's been with his mother since our divorce, but I tried to keep in touch and see him as often as I could. I never knew, never even suspected what was going on with him. It just never occurred to me that he was lonely, afraid or without hope."

Roy's son is not the only one. He survived, but how many will die by their own hands before you finish reading this page?

Teenage suicide is an epidemic in America.

Loneliness, fear, fatalism, hopelessness and cynicism run rampant in high school and college age young people today. You may be one of them.

Loneliness and being alone are two entirely different things.

Being alone is sometimes necessary, healthy, desirable and appreciated.

Loneliness never is.

That's the reason for so many singles clubs, friendship centers and dating services.

Friends are the antidote to loneliness.

"To belong" is one of the four basic desires a man has. He needs it, seeks after it, and finds satisfaction from it.

Friends are Heaven's riches.

Finding acceptance seems always to require initiation. People are intitiated into clubs, fraternities, smoking and sex. The initiation can be painful, humiliating, exhilarating, exciting or depressing, depending upon the rejection or acceptance.

Overcoming rejection is one of life's greatest feats. Salesmen understand it, writers suffer with it, people who audition accept it, and lovers live with it.

Rejection has proven to be one of the root causes of teenage suicide in America. In a society where only winners are accepted, and winning is touted as the sole criteria for self-worth, to lose is to bear a stigma of rejection which is insufferable, painful, emotionally wrenching and often devastating.

Healing is vital.

The ministry of the Lord Jesus Christ to the human heart is to heal completely the trauma of loneliness, losing and any form of rejection. When you are ministered to by the Lord with His healing, His acceptance, His power and His grace for your life, it gives you the ability to face the world and its reality. It gives you a security the world cannot match nor understand.

Jesus gives a peace, an inner stability, that is a mystery to the world but a comfort to the believer. You can trust God's Spirit in you to bring that peace from the nature of Christ into your life as needed.

But you must be yielded to the Spirit in every area of your life to experience peace. Holding on to any sin will create confusion that will keep you from experiencing peace.

Because of an intense desire to belong, to be accepted among peers, there is always the pressure to go along and do as they do in order to be one of the boys.

It isn't a phenomena that occurs only with teenagers. You read what Jeb Magruder wrote about the professional men in Watergate.

The three Hebrew children had peer pressure: If they didn't bend and bow, they would burn. They chose to burn rather than be intimidated into bending.

Make people bend to your godly standard of behavior, not you to theirs. Be the head and not the tail.

When you allow yourself to be intimidated into what your mind and heart know is wrong, you weaken your resolve to do right and impair your decision-making ability. The power of things you yield to in life grows stronger, while what you resist grows weaker.

The more you say yes to things that are right in life, the stronger you become and the greater power you have to say no.

Success in life comes from being able to say no, not the ability to say yes.

When our Lord Jesus Christ faced temptation, He overcame it through quoting the Word of God to the devil. He didn't just say no, but was able to give the reason for saying it. The devil departed and left Jesus alone. Then the Bible says Jesus "returned in the power of the Spirit."

His submission to the Father, resistance to the devil and refusal to sin strengthened His spirit and added stature to His manhood. In addition, He had memorized vast portions of scripture that gave weight to His words.

The principle applies to all of life, not just your Christian walk. If you want to succeed, you have to say no.

Many are the men who said yes to friends throughout their early manhood, when they were invited to "fool around" instead of doing what they knew was right. They knew in their hearts they should practice the piano or horn, or do homework, but they went with their friends. Saying no to friends would have enabled them to say yes to their talent and intelligence.

Today they wish they had made that right decision, because they never did learn to play the piano or horn, or they didn't graduate.

If you walked away from where you are right now and questioned the first 20 people you saw, I would guess that 19 of them, if not all 20, would admit they *wanted* to develop a talent but *didn't* because they said yes to something else.

Life would be different for most men today if they had learned and obeyed this principle when they were young. God is giving you this opportunity to learn it now and do it right.

Don't waste your youth.

The choice is yours.

The freedom to choose between alternatives is the only true freedom you have.

It is your only real freedom, so use it wisely.

You cannot choose your brothers or sisters; you can only choose to accept or reject them.

However, you can choose to graduate, play a musical instrument, be wise or ignorant, be a success or a failure. The choice is yours. Your choice.

You may not be able to choose your classmates, fellow workers, or relatives — but you can choose your friends.

You choose to go to Heaven or Hell by your choice to be a friend or an enemy of Jesus. You choose whether or not to be a real man. Your choices. Yours alone.

Your choices are shown in the company you keep.

Show me a man's companions, and I'll show you his character.

David was a young boy when I first met his parents. As he grew up in the church, he had a hunger for God and a heart that was open to receive the Word. But when he reached his teen years, he began to desire the approval of his peers more than the approval of God. He made friends with those who were merely church-wise, "Christianettes" at best, but who had no intention of ever becoming men of God. Living for themselves, they taught David to live for himself as well.

David had shown a great ability to play baseball from his childhood, but since his friends didn't play he gave up the game. Later he joined his friends in taking drugs, filling his lungs with cigarette smoke and fooling around with older girls. Today he is grown and married with two lovely children, but he is the first to admit that he could have really "been someone" had it not been for his desire for peer recognition and the approval of his church-wise friends.

You see, the church-wise need God's saving grace in their lives as much as the street-wise. Without it both suffer the same fate.

Look at the characteristics of the church-wise and street-wise:

Street-wise	**Church-wise**
Profane	Religious
Hard of heart	Hard of heart
Con parents	Con parents
Manipulative	Manipulative
Do things to impress	Do things to impress
Deceptive in spirit	Deceptive in spirit
Insolent in manner	Insolent in manner

The only real difference between them is that one is religious while the other is profane.

The church-wise are not those who genuinely love God, who earnestly seek after righteousness and desire to have their lives conform to the Word of God.

The church-wise are the men, and women, who have grown up in church, have all the cultural mannerisms and status symbols, use church slang, know church patterns, but do not have a vital living relationship with the Lord Jesus Christ.

Church-wise guys, so smug in their self-righteous attitudes, are really a stench in the nostrils of God, a pain to the pastor, a reproach to the church, and a threat to the girls.

Woe to the young lady who marries one. Without a change of heart he'll make her life a hell on earth.

That's not harsh language, that's just the truth.

We are so used to living with confusion, division and rebellion, we often forget that God has none of it in Heaven. Only obedient spirits will be allowed into Heaven. One disobedient spirit in Heaven would break the peace, and it would no longer be Heaven.

That's why it is so important for you to learn about companionships, and the contagion of sin.

Purity is not popular in most places today, but it is always the rule of the day in Heaven. If it is popular in Heaven, then the closest thing we can get to Heaven on earth is making it popular in our lives right here and now.

No wonder it is written, "Keep thyself pure."

God looks on the heart, not the facade.

If you recognize yourself as one of those church-wise people, I have one word for you that will change your life from a living hell to a living Heaven: — REPENT!

If you are not one of those, but you have befriended the church-wise crowd, looked for acceptance and approval from them, yet in your heart you want to be a man of God, do as I've said before in this book — *get away from them!*

Like begets like.

The common bond of rebels is their guilt.

Hear what God says about companionships:

"Be not deceived, evil companions corrupt good manners (lifestyle) . . .

"He that walketh with wise men shall be wise, but a companion of fools shall be destroyed."

God never says anything without a reason. He says what He means and means what He says.

The lesson of Haggai the prophet to the nation of Judah is one which we all need to learn:

Sin is contagious, righteousness is not.

Why should you waste your youth, manhood, and life caring about peer pressure from "church-wise" people who are abysmally ignorant of the true life in Christ? They are not worth living with, much less dying for.

Sure, you may have to go through the fire of persecution, be ridiculed, mocked or rejected. But remember the Hebrews who were threatened: Bend, bow or burn. They chose to go to the fiery furnace. The "fourth man," Jesus, was with them all the way and delivered them without even the smell of smoke left on them.

Fire purifies ore and strengthens steel. The fire you go through will purify and strengthen you.

Make or break, the choice is yours.

Invest your life, don't squander it.

Make Jesus your friend, not your enemy.

Make sure your friends have also made Jesus their friend.

Friendship is normal to life.

Friendship is normal in a relationship with girls and young women.

Many young men feel guilty about women because they are afraid if they date, they will be under pressure to have sex. True.

But it is also true that many young women would rather simply have a man as a friend, and let it develop into a relationship where he could become a husband.

Many men and women marry without first becoming friends. After marriage they are lovers, but still not friends. What you need to realize so you don't make that mistake is that friendship, not sex, holds a marriage together.

Between times of romance and passion, they must find a compatibility and friendship to make the marriage work.

Friends are something you make.

The common bond of friends is their trust.

If you find it difficult to make friends, or difficult to find someone you can trust, you can still become friends with God and ask Him to find other friends for you with whom you can satisfy your need of belonging.

Moses had a friendship with God.

The greatness of their friendship was not that Moses trusted God, but that God trusted Moses.

Think of it.

The basic right of society is the right of possession. From that comes the right of expectation.

When my son came home from school with his report card, and I wondered why he didn't have better grades, he asked me, "What did you expect?"

Because I provided him with all the necessities of life, a system of education, the opportunity to study, I expected in return good grades. I had the right to expect them.

He had the right to expect me to provide for him, and I had the right to expect something from him. It's a two-way street.

It's true with God also.

When we receive Jesus Christ as our Savior and come to know our heavenly Father personally, we have the right to expect that He will take care of us, provide for us, and bring us peace. By the same rules, God has the right to expect something from us.

What He expects from you is *manhood.*

He expects you to produce what you were created to be.

God desires to be intimate with you because He made it possible through Jesus Christ, Who cleansed us from the sin that separated us from God.

But intimacy and friendship are based on trust. How can God show Himself as a friend to us if we don't trust Him?

And how can God befriend us if He can't trust us?

You cannot have friendship with God through religion, but only through relationship. That relationship is based on trust, like all other friendships.

Barnabas and Paul were friends, but when John Mark failed the test in missionary work and went back home, Paul no longer trusted him. But Barnabas continued to trust Mark.

When Barnabas wanted to take Mark with them on their next trip, Paul refused because of that mistrust. The disagreement became so severe that Paul left without either of them.

Mark went with Barnabas, and we never hear about Barnabas again. But if Barnabas had not trusted Mark, even through the disagreement with Paul the Apostle, we would not have the Gospel of Mark today.

You need people you can trust to be your friends.

And you need people to trust you to fulfill your potential.

To have them, you must be trustworthy.

Be faithful to friends, keep their confidences, work for their good and enjoy their company. That means giving yourself and being willing to inconvenience yourself for them.

I had a friend once who really wanted to serve God. Rick loved being around me and the others in our ministry, and we loved him in return. But Rick had a cigarette habit that either he refused to break or felt he couldn't break. It caused him to feel uncomfortable around the rest of us without the habit. Everytime he smoked, he felt guilty. None of us said anything, but nevertheless the guilt ate at him.

He started to show up less and less and began to find unsaved friends who smoked like him. Slowly but surely, he began to live according to the lifestyle of those he befriended. Now he doesn't even have the desire to be with God's people or with God. A different kind of suicide.

It's silly to give up so much because of refusal to break a habit.

It's stupid to let that lack of ruthlessness with a habit cost you your friends, and even your soul.

God looks on the heart. If we give our all to Him, He will enable us to overcome anything that hinders us from becoming His friends.

Again, it's a matter of choice.

Choose to be a friend of God.

Be trustworthy in your manhood.

Don't succumb to the depressing entrapment of loneliness, but find solace and comfort in the peace that comes from a relationship with God that is ongoing, ever-growing, enriching you from day to day as you spend time with Him.

You need to satisfy your sense of belonging. Belong to God. Become His friend now, and grow into ever-increasing friendship with Him.

Don't waste your youth.

Don't give up your life because of loneliness. God is right there with you.

WRITE IT ON YOUR SHORTS

9

WRITE IT ON YOUR SHORTS

The meeting we were in had been intense, serious and challenging to the men there. When the call was given to be men of God, the aisles and altar area were full of men, each with their own past lives and lost dreams. But now they were going to change. They were making their commitment to be men of God.

Many of them, however, needed help in specific problems and sins they had not been able to conquer. There were counselors circulating, ministering and praying with those who wanted individual help. One man stopped me to ask for help and advice about a particular problem.

"Mr. Cole," he said, "I heard God call me into the ministry recently, and I know it was real. God told me that He would prosper me and make me an effective minister of the Gospel if I would just follow two commandments. He didn't give me 10, He just gave me two."

"And what are they, sir?" I asked.

"Well, He told me not to drink. And because I'm single, He told me not to have sex. But ever since He told me that, it seems like I've had more problems with those two sins than ever before."

"Did you write down what God told you?" I asked.

"No, sir, I didn't," he said.

"Did you know you were supposed to write down everything God tells you in order to become effective in your life?" I asked.

"Yes, sir."

"Then why didn't you write them down?"

"Well, I didn't have anything to write them in; I don't know where to write them," he said as an excuse.

"Son," I said, smiling, "why don't you write them on your shorts!"

In the intensity of the moment, the humor escaped me. But to remember the shocked expression on his face now makes me laugh that I could have said that!

Words are powerful. They are the only creative power man has.

The power of life and death are in the tongue. For that reason, we must learn to study every word God says, either through the Bible, or in our own prayer time.

Three little words, "I love you," can cause kings to abdicate their thrones, women to surrender their virtue, boys to do handstands or to work from sunup to sundown.

Nothing can compare with those three words when they are spoken from the heart.

But there are three other words that can change a man's life, making it into something it couldn't be without them. They come from Proverbs. When you apply them, they will not only make you wise but successful. They are the same three words I told that man:

Write it down.

The difference between David and Saul was not only that David loved truth, and Saul didn't; it was that David loved truth enough to write down everything God told him, and Saul didn't. By neglect, Saul defaulted on his leadership and forfeited his kingdom.

To this day we sing the psalms of David. They are words recorded under the inspiration of God's Spirit and still bring life to those who hear them. Saul is long gone. He is merely an example of error in the book of divine history. He never wrote down the works of the Lord.

There would be no book at all if the men of God had not been trained by God to write down His revelation and truth as it came to their hearts and minds. Those men who wrote the Bible blessed heaven and earth because of their faithfulness.

When David reached the lowest point of his career, when everyone he had loved and trusted seemed to have turned against him, he was able to strengthen himself by reading all that God had done for him before that time. The Bible actually says, "He strengthened himself in the Lord." Just by reading the words, he was able to turn around and become completely victorious. In the strength of those words, he recaptured his family and his men, then went on to capture the kingdom as well.

There is no way these words can be minimized.

Write it down!

The core of ignorance is stubbornness. A stubborn man who refuses to be taught will always be ignorant. Ignorant men will always be at the mercy of the knowledgeable.

One of the great tragedies of our day is the number of men who finished high school and college only because they passed tests but never learned anything that lasts. They failed to retain because they only studied to pass the tests, not to learn.

Passing tests is not a sign of learning.

In fact, on most college campuses you can buy answers to test questions so you don't even need to cram for tests in order to graduate.

What a waste!

Waste of time. Waste of money. Waste of energy. Waste of a mind.

Prisons are full of men who have never learned. So are our civil courts. And so are our hospitals.

The men who applied themselves to learn are the presidents of large corporations, doctors, statesmen and lawyers. They not only retained what they were taught, but they applied it and became successful. Not all of them may have learned what they know today by a formal education, but they learned how to learn, then they learned what they needed to know to become successful. Knowing how to learn, knowing where to find answers and having good reading skills are all important to becoming a success.

It's true with ministers. Some only read the Bible to get sermons. They don't read it in order to learn it, to apply it and then to live it. But God didn't give His Word simply to be read, it is meant to be *lived*.

You must discipline yourself to learn. Learning doesn't come by natural inclination or by mistake.

All discipline is based on preference.

Men who win gold medals don't punish their bodies in practice because they hate themselves, but because they *prefer* to win.

Discipline is the correct application of pressure. One of the tests of manhood is how a man handles pressure.

"You are a poor specimen if you can't stand the pressure of adversity," the Bible tells us in Proverbs.

Boot camps, cadet corps, apprenticeships and initiations are all times when men are tested under adversity to determine their ability to behave right under pressure.

An innate weakness may disqualify them. The men must be tested and proven before they can be given authority.

Whether college or boot camp, it is all discipline. The things you study are called disciplines.

Many men who go to church regularly have trained themselves for the wrong thing. They are trained to hear sermons, not study the Word of God. Look around you and see how many men bring their Bibles with them, ready to open them and receive the Word into their lives.

In church youth groups, how many are there to learn the Word of God? How many are there to be discipled?

God said in His Word not to despise His Word — that means not to neglect it. Yet time after time people hear but don't do. Even though they say "amen" to the scripture that says, "Be doers of the Word and not hearers only," they still don't do, they just "amen" it.

Don't be deceived. That is not an example for you to follow.

Don't waste your youth.

Don't waste what God gives you.

Write it down!

One of the reasons men repeat mistakes and never learn from them is that they never took the time to record them for their own personal good. The same man might write down his profit and loss statement in business, and pay close attention to it to learn from it, yet he neglects to write down what God is teaching him.

It makes the difference. It is being a steward of God's Word instead of despising it.

You must learn to keep a notebook and pencil handy. Particularly when you pray or read the Word, have that notebook and pencil ready for God to speak to you. I am adamant about this with those who work for me. Everyone is required to come to meetings with a notebook and pencil at all times.

Burt was a bright young guy who came to work for me and really showed promise. He seemed to have everything going for him; however, he was ineffective. I finally saw the pattern.

Every time we came together, or I gave him instructions privately, he didn't write them down. Time and time again he made the same mistakes, but he never learned to write things down. His excuse was that he'd do it later, or he had it written down but couldn't find it, or that he didn't have his pad of paper right now, it was at home, in the car, in the desk — never with him.

That one lack of discipline is still costing him years of effective ministry. He is working somewhere else, still has the same potential but has yet to fulfill it.

Mike was another young man who came to work with the ministry. He wrote down everything I ever said. He wrote down things I said in men's meetings, church services, staff meetings, in the car and in restaurants. He was like an encyclopedia of my teachings. He kept notebooks full of everything. He kept a pencil poised, waiting for me to say the next word.

While he was diligent in writing it, he didn't love the Word; therefore, he didn't apply it to his life. He was keeping it, as if one day he miraculously would live by all he had learned. He didn't discipline himself to start living it, applying it immediately.

Everything in life is subject to discipline.

Even you.

The rules for correction in the home or on the job are generally: Punish in private, reward in public.

Parents have come up with "tough love" to deal with the drug addict and run-away child. It's simply the act of drawing the lines of discipline. Children are confused by their parents' behavior when the lines have never been drawn for them.

Lines drawn on the highway are not an evidence of someone who wants to keep you from being an independent thinker; they are there to keep you from killing yourself. It's not someone with governmental power trying to be mean to everyone else; it's a necessary discipline.

Anarchy is the rebellion against such laws and the effort to remove them. It is the refusal to accept authority.

The Bible calls anarchy lawlessness and says it is one of the signs of the spirit of Antichrist in the earth.

Tough love is the only kind of love God knows. It is love that endures even when you are wrong and strives to keep you right. God draws lines to give us boundaries for our lives so that we won't be killed by sin.

A man came to me asking for advice regarding his son. Matt had been bringing home his girlfriend regularly, and they spent a lot of time alone in his bedroom. Now Matt wanted to bring her home for the weekend.

"Mr. Cole, what should I do?" he asked. "I love my son, and he tells me I don't really love him because I don't want him bringing her over for the weekend. He accuses me of not being a good Christian because I won't let him do it."

"Sir," I said, "you have created your own problem because, number one, you have not been living a strong Christian life at home. Number two, you have allowed your son to do whatever he wanted because of your weakness. And number three, you have lost all respect and authority and cannot take a stand at this time.

"What you are going to have to do is pray with your wife, come into agreement on it, and then tell your son that in order to live under your roof, he is going to have to live by your standards."

Hard? Tough? Matt's father thought so!

But how can that father justify a son who is disrupting the family by bringing his sins and lack of respect into the home? Matt's father wants what is best for him. God wants what is best for him. It is best that Matt learn to accept authority now when he is young, instead of being forced to accept it someday in prison or after failing in job after job.

The Proverbs say, "It is senseless to pay tuition to educate a rebel who has no heart for truth."

That's been our problem in America. We have indulged the rebel in his rebellion. Consequently, there are a lot of men older than you who have never lived to their full potential because they were indulged early in their lives.

Like the prodigal who said, "Give me," and then finally said, "Make me," repentance is the pivotal point between ruin and reconciliation. All rebels have to reach that point before they can become restored to their full potential.

Discipline. You must have discipline for your own sake, not just for others.

There are three things men across the country are learning in motivational seminars today:

Decision. Dedication. Discipline.

All decisions translate into energy. Remember what the Word says about a double-minded man. He doesn't have the energy to accomplish anything because he has not made a decision. Decisions motivate you to action.

Once a decision is made, it takes dedication to reach the goal of that decision. Against adversity and the toughest odds, men throughout history have been known to achieve their goals because of their dedication. They also had discipline, or they would not have made it.

But there is a fourth element that is often overlooked yet is often the crucial element that determines the success or failure of the other three.

Details.

At home, school and work, young men fail and make mistakes because of their lack of attention to details. Whether in your English class with grammar, at home with the clutter in your room, or at work with those little requirements that endear you to — or alienate you from — your boss, details make the difference between success and failure.

Learn that now.

In fact, write it down!

Take a washable marker and write it on your mirror, so every morning you remember to take care of details. For the rest of your life you will be grateful for that one word — details.

God is so concerned with details that He says even the hairs of our heads are numbered. You can look through a microscope and see the concern God has for details.

The difference between a large company and a small one is generally not the talent, but the attention given to details. It's the same with a ball team or a club.

It's also true in a marriage.

Jerry was the focal point of a business when it first began and started growing. But since the business has grown to a multi-million-dollar company today, Jerry is no longer with them. He had to leave because he couldn't grow with the company. Why? He never learned how to attend to details. How should someone attend to details? Write them down!

Jerry could have stayed and become a member of the executive staff, but he thought he could remember everything he needed to know. No one can remember it all. You have to learn to write down the details.

That's the reason some men sleep soundly at night, and others are restless. The restless ones have their minds so filled with clutter it bothers them all night long. There's a simple formula for that:

On the paper — off the mind.

That's why taking notes in class is so important. It is impossible to listen to two or three lectures a day and then pass a test. No man can remember all that! It is simply idiotic.

Some young men turn off to education because they never learned how to learn. The secret is simple, and it really requires very little effort.

Just write it down.

Laziness is a sin, the Bible tells us.

The guy who won't write it down because it is too much trouble is just plain lazy. Laziness of mind is common, but it is still sinful. The tragedy is that so many men won't admit the sin.

Procrastination is a form of laziness.

Laziness and dumbness go hand in hand.

"The lazy man is brother to the saboteur," the Word says.

In Matthew 25:14-30, Jesus gives a parable about how each man invested his money, and about the one who didn't invest it but buried it instead. Those who invested got great returns for their efforts, but the man who buried it lost everything. He was too lazy and too afraid and too dumb to work with it.

It is interesting that the principle Jesus gave us then is still working today.

The man who does the least, talks the most.

He tries to cover his failure with excuses, but they are unacceptable.

Excuses are not reasons.

Lazy men, unfaithful men and unproductive men offer all kinds of excuses to cover their failures.

Successful men can let their work do the talking for them.

Decision. Dedication. Discipline. Details.

You must write them down. When you make a decision, write it down so you are motivated to hold to it. Dedicate yourself to your goals and have the discipline to reach them. Pay attention to details and, by all means, write down every important thing that happens.

Above all, for the man who wants to become God's man, apply those principles to your Christian walk.

Decide to be a man of God. Write it down. Dedicate yourself to that goal and begin faithfully studying God's Word. Write down everything God tells you. Make notes in your Bible or in a special notebook to remember what the Lord tells you about specific scriptures.

Have the discipline to be a "doer" and not just a "hearer." Discipline yourself to do what God tells you to do.

Commit yourself to it in writing and in prayer. Remember, "An ounce of obedience is worth a pound of prayer."

Have the discipline of obedience working in your life — not procrastination, but immediate obedience.

Then, when times are tough, you will have a wealth of written words to encourage you. You will know God is going to move in your behalf, because you will see when God has helped you before.

Be a David, not a Saul. Make a mark in history; don't be an example of what not to do.

Discipline yourself.

Write it down.

Don't waste your youth.

Write down today what God has taught you.

CHAMPIONS: MEN WHO NEVER QUIT

10
CHAMPIONS: MEN WHO NEVER QUIT

In a meeting recently, I watched many young men answer the call for commitment to Christ, and take their stand before hundreds of people. After the meeting, one young man approached me and quietly addressed me after everyone else left.

"I wanted to take my stand, too," he said, "but I was afraid I would fail."

I took him by the hand and led him in the prayer of commitment because there was one thing he had failed to understand.

Champions are not those who never fail, they are those who never quit.

Fear of failure is no reason for lack of commitment. Failures and setbacks may occur, but the champion holds out for his goal.

Men love winners. They want to be identified with winners.

Men open a newspaper and turn directly to the sports page because it features winners, while the front page usually features losers.

Millions of advertising dollars are spent using winners to attract buyers to their products. You see winners on boxes of cereal, selling insurance, eating foods, driving cars; you see their names on shoes, clothes and sporting equipment; you see them standing in their underwear on the pages of magazines. Buy this underwear if you want to be a winner, is what they are saying. Sounds silly, but what do we do? Buy it. Why? Because we love winners!

But the difference between the top money winner and the 10th-place finisher on the professional golf tour is only three-tenths of a stroke.

At the Olympics, the difference between first and second, gold and silver, is measured in hundredths of an inch, thousandths of a second, and fractions of a point.

You can be only a breath away from winning, but not win. You can be rejoicing that you escaped from the sink, but be going down the drain.

Champions are the right man, in the right place, at the right time. Timing is all important.

God has an eternal clock which was started from the beginning of time to make you become a champion for Him.

To become a champion, you must see yourself as a champion.

Hanging on to the fear of failure, the sins of others and past mistakes will keep you from becoming a champion.

Champions are made, not born.

Many champions start with severe handicaps in life, but in making the effort to overcome, they find the ability to continue until they have excelled beyond those even without handicaps.

Champions are men in whom courage has become visible.

Reading the Bible will teach you about champions. In fact, the Word says that some were so noble, the world was not worthy of them. Men grew to such stature that God acknowledged them as great even in His eyes.

But then, God encourages you to be the same, and He promises to look at you the same way.

Don't waste your youth.

God spoke to one young man and said, *"You could have had more, but you settled for less."*

Your choice. You do the choosing.

The athlete, the farmer and the soldier all have different ways of winning. Each of them does his training, plowing or exercising in private, and they show their abilities in public.

It's what you do when you are alone that determines if you will win or lose.

Each of them knows the price that has to be paid in order to win. You need to learn it, too.

No gain without pain.

The fainthearted never win, they wilt. They start well, but fade before they finish. Looking good at the start means nothing, but looking good at the finish means everything. Don't worry about an embarrassing start.

Don't let others despise your youth.

You can make a decision, but determination carries it through. That is how you become a champion, a member of God's "Championship Team."

The Rev. Dick Mills has an excellent word for you. It's taken from the Bible and deals with that word, "man." Here are the four root words of man:

ADAM is the generic Hebrew root for man (mankind) as distinguished from animals. ADAM primarily means MAN IN RELATIONSHIP to God and to God's creation. As such, he is blessed of God and, most importantly, ADAM is *UNIQUE*.

ISH is the word for man as male, individual, person, husband, man of courage and man of word.

ENOSH is the word for man as a weak, feeble, fragile and moral being. Enough of ENOSH.

GEBER is the word used of man as a male, as a mature adult, and as hero. The word contains the element of strength that comes from superiority and/or maturity.

The word designated for the expected Messiah in Isaiah 9:6 is EL GIBBOR (from the root word, GEBER). It is usually translated "Mighty God," but more exactly it is "Powerful Champion" or "Godly Hero."

The word GEBER is used when the Bible tells about the fourth man in the fiery furnace with the three Hebrew children. Together with God, they made up the championship team which braved the sentence of death and came out victorious.

Men who belong to God are to be members of a championship team and treat each other as such. They are to be the GEBER of modern times, joined with their Lord, the mighty, powerful Champion of Champions.

There are members of God's championship team whom I have met and whom I am proud to admit, "I'm one of them." Others have called themselves teammates but they were unable to produce the fruits of the Spirit because they refused to walk after the Spirit, and they were cut from the team.

That's why the Bible says there are some vessels to honor, some to dishonor.

Casey Treat was a teenager on the street, into drugs and finally into a drug rehabilitation center. His counselor told Casey about the Lord Jesus Christ. Casey made his commitment to the Lord, but determined not only to live for God, but to be as bold for the Lord in his new life as he was for sin in the old.

As Casey applied himself to study God's Word, he grew in stature and in favor with God and man. By honoring God, he brought honor to himself. Within a few years he began a church with 25 people. That was five years ago. Today it has a congregation of 3,000 and is still growing. Casey did all that while still in his 20s.

I'm proud to be on Casey's team.

Jim appeared on the *700 Club* television program recently to tell how things in his high school had become so bad that he decided to do something about it. He saw himself as student body president, having others around him who were all out for God and changing his school. Rather than being intimidated by others, he made the decision to be an influence on them.

Everything Jim envisioned, he prayed for and worked toward. He saw those things happen. He is known nationally today as a single high school student who made the difference.

I'm proud to be on Jim's team.

The two sons of a pastor friend of mine were having problems in their lives. Busy with the church, radio station and other activities, the pastor thought everything was great — until they were arrested.

He was shocked, hurt and disappointed, but he realized something had to be done. *He* had to do it.

The pastor took a six-month leave of absence from everything he was doing to give his undivided attention to his sons, to help them in their time of crisis. Nothing was more important to him than for his sons to have a dad who cared and showed it.

I'm proud to be on that pastor's team.

In Houston, Doug had a physical fitness center when he gave his life to the Lord. Telling his customers about the Lord began to take so much of his time that he turned it into a youth center to help troubled young people.

Doug made every effort to tell his family about the Lord. Finally, he traveled across the country to see them and led every family member to Christ. They are now living lives changed by the power of God because of his testimony.

I'm proud to be on Doug's team.

Joe was a football fanatic, a sports enthusiast and participant. More than anything he wanted to play professional ball, but living for drugs, sex and pleasure took its toll, and he never made it. Then one night he heard the command to repent and believe on the Lord Jesus Christ. He did.

Today he tells everyone he meets that homosexuality, drugs and all that goes with it are "not where it's at," but that Jesus is "where it's at."

Eloquent or not, I'm proud to be on Joe's team.

We're all members of the same team, the championship team of God, and we're proud of it and of each other.

Whether athlete, farmer or soldier, we're members of the same team. We all train alone, but we all have in mind the goal God has set for us personally to attain. Whether it's a medal, a crop or a battle victory, it is for God's glory and His purpose with His team.

Ananias of Damascus lived a life of righteousness and devotion to the Lord, but you only see his name in the Bible for one thing he accomplished. No one knew much about Ananias except the Lord. When it came time to have someone who God could depend on, He chose Ananias.

The only thing we know about him is that he knew God's voice, heard it, and in obedience went and prayed for the man who would later become the Apostle Paul to receive his sight.

We never hear of him again.

The right man, in the right place, at the right time.

Like an Olympic champion who only wins one race, then goes on to live a regular life, but has his name live on in history. That was Ananias.

A champion — a member of the championship team — Ananias accomplished God's goal for him to achieve one great thing in his life, and it affected everyone in the world from that time until this.

I'm proud to be on his team.

Joshua was a member of the championship team.

He could hardly stand to see other men who didn't feel the way he did, and finally issued the challenge that lives on forever.

"Choose this day whom you will serve, but as for me and my house, *we will serve the Lord.*"

I'm proud to be on Joshua's team.

You are a member of a championship team, or can be. God has called you to be a champion.

That's why this book was written, so that one day someone else will say about you:

"I'm proud to be on his team."

Don't waste your youth.

Choose the more excellent way.

Be the man God wants you to be:

A MAN OF GOD.

A CHAMPION!

PUBLISHER'S AFTERWORD

Many of the problems that we as a society face today result directly from a lack of godly leadership of young men. That is the reason why we have released this special limited edition of *Courage — Winning Life's Toughest Battles.* We at Harrison House are deeply concerned with the future of our nation and the young men who will lead it one day.

Bound in a special desert-camouflage look, this limited edition has been produced to send to the men and women who are serving in the United States Armed Services' Operation "Desert Storm." Our prayers are with these men and women, and we believe that this outstanding and inspiring book will motivate them on to greater heights.

Now that you have read this inspirational charge from Edwin Louis Cole, we encourage you to act on it. Stand up and be the man God wants you to be. Be a champion!

From preteen to teen-men to adults, men have testified to the validity of the truths of this book and the life-changing power inside. I gratefully thank those who have made it possible.

As a veteran myself, I thank the brave men and women of our Armed Forces for all you have done for me, my family, and for America. Most of all, I salute you, young man, for having the courage to pick up this book, read it, and take it to heart. You are our future. May God richly bless you and our nation through you.

EDWIN LOUIS COLE —

Internationally acclaimed speaker, television personality, best-selling author and motivational lecturer, known for his practical application of wisdom from kingdom principles.

Ed Cole has been called to speak with a prophetic voice to men, challenging them to fulfill their potential for true manhood, which is Christlikeness. He now travels extensively, exhorting young men to realize their dreams by disciplining themselves to God's favor, wisdom and courage.

To receive Edwin Louis Cole's publication, *COURAGE,* write:

EDWIN LOUIS COLE MINISTRIES
P. O. Box 610588
Dallas, Texas 75261

Other Books
By Edwin Louis Cole

Communication, Sex and Money

Maximized Manhood

The Potential Principle

Invest to Increase

The Sacredness of Sex

When Life is Just Too Tough

Entering Crisis and Leaving

The Unique Woman
Co-Authored by Nancy Cole

Available at your local bookstore.

Harrison House
P. O. Box 35035
Tulsa, OK 74153